THE GREATEST GIFT

by

ANGUS PETER CAMPBELL

i

Published by:
Fountain Publishing
Sabhal Mòr Ostaig
Teangue
Sleat
Isle of Skye
IV44 8RQ

Typeset in Novarese by Saxon Graphics, Derby;
Cover printed by Highland Printers, Inverness;
Text by Bookcraft, Bath.

ISBN 0-9620010-0-4

The author would like to give particular thanks to the Scottish Arts Council, Keith Murray Publishing, Sabhal Mor Ostaig and Christian Focus Publications for help towards publishing this book.

Preface

I have known Angus Peter Campbell for a long time and am very pleased that he is now able to bring together so many poems for a book.

I have read the poems with great interest. They are very varied – some about his daughter, some about his beloved Highlands, some about Edinburgh, some about deprivation in a callous Thatcherite (and now post-Thatcherite) world.

These latter in particular are very moving, and powerful, and the cry about poverty in them is an authentic cry. HUMAN RIGHTS and BINS are very evocative. This, one believes, is the voice of someone who suffered and was there. This cry is joined with the cry against the oppression of his own people, against apartheid, against starvation in Ethiopia and so on. These poems are from a spirit whose vulnerable sensitivity will not let it rest.

It is the voice of one who knows the history of his own people and who will refer to them in a familiar way. Poems too about his father are very moving, and especially the ones for his daughter who becomes a precious symbol in a terrible world.

For Angus Peter the solution to the ills of the world lies in Christ, and here too he is authentic and sincere.

I find this book, as I have said, very moving, in its openness to the world, in its pity for the wounded and the hurt, in its contempt for the uncaringness of Thatcherism, and other equally harsh ideologies, in its stare into the abyss, and also in its lyric moments.

Angus Peter is currently Writer-in-Residence at Sabhal Mor Ostaig in Skye, where I am sure he is doing much for the Gaelic language and its arts. I hope that he will also continue with his own poetry of which this book is the first fruits.

I am delighted to have been asked to write this preface.

Iain Crichton Smith.

For
Shona

Contents
Page

Uist 1958

Printed frocks are all I see
and that swift sunshine,
that swift swift sunshine.

Your hair a haystack of curls
in the Garrynamonie morning,
and a green bicycle going softly by.

Shouts, distant calls,
rusty drums and leather balls.

A peewit called,
a school bell, a square bus went by.

A gorgeous print frock by a stone wall.

Uist 1960

Cycling,
you could see them miles away
in the still haze of that Uist day.

Strangers
glittering with silver wheels
and red headbands and green pouches
and a lovely wave as they travelled on.

A soft hiss, a soft hiss,
and the sun caught the spokes as they climbed,
and the hiss, and the hiss, and the hiss,
and the hiss became a distant cow.

The Village

I see them now only in old magazines,
collars turned against the breeze,
hats askew,
the plain grass stretching around them
between curved Sunbeams and kangaroos
in that false world that portrayed them
as separate from their time, not undone
by war and poverty and the great disease
of sexism obscuring the greater pain,
dying outwith one another's arms with sighs
that the machair and the moor had altered
and that the young didn't care anymore

beyond the magazines they are in the television mind

I see horses trundling across the ridges of the moor
and sheepdogs barking on the great day of the fank
and the thin gaunt cattle being herded on a primary day
like technicolour incidents out of a John Wayne movie

to me they were just the dying old
dying whom I can now name
name by separate name
houses stretching back those seven astonishing generations
made valid by death linking grandfather and daughter,
a mediaeval incident brushing me on the cheek at the age of seven

to me they were just the dying old
for I had never seen them lay the foundation stone
or trundle with their horse and cart on the summer hillside
each with his peat, his corked bottle, his story,
that eloquent stone, that historic wall, that ancient blade of grass,
the burial place bought from the sons of Heth,

I see them now only in old magazines
in their Sunday hats and turned-up coats,
bone of my bone, flesh of my flesh,

I am Jacob gone into a foreign land
where I have spent beautiful days with Leah
Rachel with the eyes of a dove
stiller than a Highland pool
I send ahead of me all the treasures I have gathered
as I wrestle with the fierce angel of time and memory here
struggling that you will accept
that my escape was in the footsteps of God
and that I met with my father at Bethel as well as Boisdale

Esau, accept my gifts and accept me
even as you run to greet me
in tears we are back here in Canaan
surrounded by the memory of Abraham and the Celtic thought of
Columcille,
with the greater tragedy and the greater delivery
of the famine and Joseph and his separate dreams still to come

and what shall we say
of Gideon and Barak and Samson and Jephthah and David and Samuel
and the prophets who did not receive what was promised
until one day I left Boisdale and fled into exile beyond Easabhal
till I met those who were returning from the féill,
such a great cloud of circumcised witnesses
fixing their eyes on the grace of forty years,
that they too, before the magazine picture was taken,
had become Hebrews as well as Gaels.

An Inheritance

I visited you often
and you told me stories
of the burning of the kelp
and how the giants had constructed the causeway

and I took your cattle up on the high hill
and when there was a window needing repaired
I repaired it.

Johnny leaning on your cas-chrom
I see you at the end of your house
leaning between history and extinction

that evening you offered me your croft
and all that you had in your universe
your silver pocket watch found at Arras
and your stirk and hens and byre and fields
and the great bardic poetry honeyed in your head
and your love for the church
and each knoll where we sat each summer
talking of nothing in particular

my son writes these lines
from the vast urban inheritance that has fallen on him

your croft lies roofless and in ruins
for I did not accept the unconditional offer you made
and now I lie in Halainn hill and you beside me
finally sharing that inheritance
that I now unconditionally bestow
on her.

Daliburgh

Burnt, the air was burning,
you were burning,
somewhere you were burning
burning around me
burning with that sweetness
of the forbidden,
the forbidden.

Someone spoke a word
and you were in it
somewhere
somewhere
at the edge of the school house
yet not there, not there.

He talked of you again
and I caught
that vast skirted image
of a name, Mary,
yes maybe Mary
and the pier on which you kissed
that early summer night
when the moor burned
with your name, yet not your name
yet not your name.

Home on Leave

We recently found a wooden board on which my late father, a
joiner, had written, in pencil, in 1940:

> *Ewen Campbell. Age 30 Yrs working on this house. home on*
> *leave. after being working*
> *Harland & Wolf. Govan Glasgow*
> *date. 24 October 1940 war time*
> *if I'm living when this board traced*
> *up. please let me know if dead*
> *pray. for my soul and offer*
> *mass, on my behalf*

Now: Angus Peter Campbell, age 36 years,
working on this poem, here in Edinburgh,
28 March 1989; if this poem found in 2038
and I am still alive, please let me know;
if dead, you will remember your own mortality

and add nothing for nothing can be added
as I am adding nothing now to the plaque
that brought further tears to my eyes
when I remembered that you were not yet married
and I twelve years unborn when you wrote your epitaph

Shona, my love, I name you now
as the inheritor of this board of chaotic letters
that pour out of this twentieth century evening
when we can still remember cattle and green grass
and white rivers forded by rickety Highland bridges

what tubular world will encase Boisdale when
I am eighty-seven years of age and you, light
in the evening sky, an age that you are, four
now and the blueness of the sky this night
like the first laughter of your voice, then

the curlew whistling as I played football
and my father stood at the end of the long grass
urging me to run faster than the Irish west wind
tomorrow we would travel north to Howmore
and build a church and catch a trout

where the river shingle turned to gold,
an ambulance and suddenly there was marram grass
swaying amidst the generations in the sand
taken by trivialities: heart disease, cancer, the occasional accident,
now as if memory were more important than life itself

what stuns the page is the pencil grip on the hand
asserting the peace that I can only believe exists
I saw in the summer your smile wider than Loch Ness
and dragging me into the secret tent the grass
burnt grey by the canvas that hid us from the world

Ewen Campbell, age 30 years, home on leave ,
Angus Peter Campbell, age 36 years, home on leave,
Shona Campbell, age 4 years, home on leave:
the wooden board and the joiner's pencil,
the typewriter and the poem,
the sky now dark and the stunning blue somewhere in my soul.

Victory and Defeat

"You yourself must not distinguish
your victory from your defeat": Pasternak

I know those who sleep in cardboard boxes,
greeting the stunning noon of a giro
and the brief blessing of dry steps,
Nelson committing adultery and him at Trafalgar
a hero whom Thatcher would have exalted in her heart
where the prostitutes of Leith deserve their aids
as if they were any different from unfortunate Mountbatten
and him murdered by the IRA in a different land:
put that on ITN and read it as if Biblical passages
were equivalent to the Koran;

I never learned one damn thing from experience
except perhaps how to repeat the same mistakes -
Clive in India with the servile tea boys
and the cardboard boxes, the stiff medals.

There were victories - Agincourt and Bannockburn,
my MA degree (with honours), my TV job, my marriage,
the thick cardboard round the winter winds in Aberdeen,
the medals on the thrusting breast of the adulterous hero,
running like the wind across Easabhal, Madrid.

And what of failure, as Eliot might say: aye, there was that too-
my mother, me sleeping rough, those endless queues in the social
where cardboard was far more than an image,
where the medals of the DHSS shone in the evening sun.

There was a man I knew
whose arm was severed by 50,000 volts
as he tried to steal copper from the hydro board:
each morning he would leave the room
and click on his arm outside the door
for fear of waking us with the sound.

What do you know of it, Thatcher, in your graceless cabinet
where the crystal glasses shine without a single thumb print,
not even reflecting, as in a mirror, the vague image of Pilton.

There is nothing like certainty,
the powerful rule of law,
the divisions, the clarity, the divide, the political finality:
what grace you have, Margaret,
that ability to distinguish between victory and defeat,
as if Pasternak had never existed,
as if the commandments could fulfil the beatitudes.

I have seen two women
to whom morality was preached from birth
dancing in the church when they heard the sermon on the mount
the very week you preached a different gospel on the Mound.

We cannot all be as clever as you, Margaret,
or as strong or as beautiful, even with your patrician help,
and I'm really sorry, maam, that I am part of the dependency
culture
for I need the love of May and George and Gordon
more than I need the shoes in which I stand,
though they were bought with my journalistic wages.

When the whip cracks at 3am
and I lose the glorious image of your eyes
I cannot believe that I will ever see you again
and you more precious to me than every word I have ever written
can I turn to you Margaret Thatcher in my bed
and ask that you would kiss away the fears
that have made me a Gael and a socialist and a Christian

in the face of indifference and poverty and weakness
there are people who have banished the evil of self-assurance
and listed my tears on the scroll of those who oppose you
I phone him and he tells me that he cares for me
even though I have desecrated my religion
and abandoned all the things that were ever precious to me,
you included, he girds me with the giro wall of his love
and crawls ten thousand miles to fetch me a crumb
that will keep the unconquerable law at bay.

I love you you love I love I you love I you
have you ever pronounced these words upon your soft lips, Margaret,
in the soft night, when the soft moon is soft in London's soft fog,
when the cardboard is soft with rain
and the medals softened by Dali's time,
after you have made love and all is soft and gentle and sweet,
Margaret, did you even then distinguish your victory from your defeat.

Halainn Hill

They are all there tonight
in this fresh October storm:
my father, Calum beag, Rory and the ghosts
that high-pitched whistled through the gaps in the mossy dykes
especially on November nights when that north-western corner of Daliburg
was always the first to be cloaked by Atlantic darkness,
that unconscious place next to the shore, nearest to the fairy wheel-
houses,
the far place separated from village by fear -
down there dark winds howled and caped voices were heard
moaning

my God, who were they but Alastair and Donald and Alastair Iain
once smoking briar pipes against the gable end, smiling,
talking of sheep and cattle and herring and crops
and the carts going west smelling of seaweed to the thin potato fields:
are these fearful ghosts the heavy-jowled men who munched milked
potatoes,
had one suit, one shirt, one pair of shoes and maybe two saved florins
in the too brief interval between digging and digging:
are these fearful ghosts the tall thin women who raked the fire at dawn,
who cooked, washed, gave birth, gutted, sang, prayed, starved, died
in home-made beds that knew no lust, no sin of luxury

too innocent even to be ghosts
if lost souls wander beneath wild moonlights
they must be strangers to Uist, foreigners to poverty,
not resting in the peace of the bush, the peace of deprivation.

Substitute

Since there is no other love but this
this itself is love
as you recline in the imagination
of my love
my love
suckling the milk that tinkles with the perfection
that I cannot but conclude was born with you
in the eternity that is set in the hearts of men
we yearn across the inhumane chasm
that is breached by your willing ear
and the iridescent fountain of my stories
which sometimes reach that perfect point of peace
which is an incandescent pinprick of light at the tip
of your fresh touch upon the universe.

Phoning You

The many Saturday nights
I have sat here
looking through the grilled windows
waiting for that precise moment
when your bath is done
and I can plug in to that unchanging love
that has been built on this abhorrent technological miracle
that sustains my days

here in darkest Edinburgh
on this November evening
I watch the tea-time lamps being lit in Stockbridge
not daring to hear the dance music that is being played
in that sunlit house across the way

where I see a girl who was a child a year ago
sweep her hair into her father's arms

while I wait for that exact moment
that will eradicate the books unread
and redeem the crippled day that I have spent
waiting for this unfair moment
that sustains and tears our broken hearts.

Without You

It's now been a thousand nights,
smiles not seen, the croon of your pillow,
eyes lighting on a snow-filled morning,
tummy-aches, small wounds on the fingers,
waking, sleeping, walking, talking, crying,

and though I were to chisel a million words
on the million stars in this millionth sky
they could not resurrect Foinavon not seen
or the friendships sown in the glance of a season,
in the wink of any eye, in the passing of time,

a woman comes to mind, a widow, widowed now
for fifty years by war, twenty thousand nights
smiles not seen, a husband's laughter unheard
but the dull throb of the grey Atlantic convoys
a sounding-echo in her soul, an echo sounding

where words cease, inadequate to express, explain
this pain, this loss, of a husband's wedding hand,
a child's upturned hand, asleep, the possibility
of the crunch of your feet, your embrace in my arms
asleep, time, love, face, hair, voice, all nights asleep.

Your First Day At School, And Tiananmen Square

The real, selfish, pain
is that I am not there
and you so pretty this morning
in this blue dress and your bicycle by the school gate.

The others were, of course, crushed last Saturday at Tiananmen Square,
and though your first day at school is not until August
the two are together in this horror story,
here in June, in Edinburgh, again.

On the actual night I phoned you
and we played the usual story of losing ourselves in the cave:
do you have a candle, no, do you have a lamp, no, do you have a
match, no.
and oh, here comes the monster now, creeping, OH NO.

And then the endless laugh, the hollowed out hills laughing,
reverberating Drumnadrochit, scorching Morar, smiling skies:
you shout down the plug hole, just shout my name, Daddy,
and I'll shout back, Shona, Shona, where are you, where are you?

Where are you, Tiananmen Square, hiding behind the sofa -
I can see you, crushed bicycles, lunacy, Kate Adie and the bullets:
do you have a candle, no, do you have a lamp, no, do you have a
match, no,
and oh, here comes the monster now, creeping, OH NO.

The Impossible

Come through and see me in five minutes,
even though you are a hundred miles away
I will see you resurrected in the door light
like certainty descending on my dreams I
imagine that we have just played hide-and-seek
around the sure tents that surround us each day

take me high up on to that high mountain
where we are transfigured walking on the water
rebuking the wind and waves until I looked and
sank before the eternal certainty of your hand
reassured me that there was no such thing
as a separation between father and child

I gaze up where no dried wounds are required
to prove the completion of our daily love.

My Nephew's Perception Of My Father

BIG HANDS

Dancing In The Crimea

My young daughter tells me that there is dancing in the Crimea,
that Florence Nightingale is playing the pipes
and that the wounded soldiers have gathered
from Culloden and Balaclava to dance to the great tunes:
that MacCrimmon's Lament cannot be heard
because of the ecstasy of the reel to Padraig Mòr
and the beat of the great drums stirring the ankles out of the mud
where heads and arms and bayonets lie
unwanted like lined maidens in Highland halls
waiting for the drunken command
that would take them on to the crowded floor
where Bismarck is dancing with the African Queen
and the Somme and Belsen stand waiting for the waltz
that even then was not the last that would close the hall
to the endless dance that goes on and on.

I see them standing in long silent rows
waiting for the scottische of Sarajevo
and the eightsome reel of Ypres,
the dashing white sergeant of Vietnam
and the quick quickstep of the Falklands,
songs ringing across the Daliburgh skies
with the moon full over Easabhal
and the children scattered over the globe

I see that the 93rd Highland Infantry are there as usual
receding in a thin red line
even though Florence Nightingale is there
forever playing The Lament for Rory Mòr MacLeod
with all the human grace notes that she knows
the generals cry out for more and another reel begins
to the demonic spin of accordian and fiddle

like lighting Einstein is swept across the floor
to dance unwillingly with the prostitute that hangs about the door

spreading her disease into the highly musical night
she rapes him in the dark wallowing with delight

that their brief fusion has been turned into a fission
which will make her mission sparkle at the door

where the satellite camera lights upon her lovely scarlet robe
as she pouts and asks everyone to dance with her just once more

merely for the sake of procreation, she exclaims,
I need you to minister to my endless needs this night:

there is no dancing without intercourse, she proclaims,
and once the deed is done you can return to the great reel

which is spinning around those who did not return
from Sheriffmuir or from Nagasaki
despite the great tunes that were playing in their heads
and the beautiful nurses who attended to the wounds
of some who managed a brief step or two from the frozen field
before death saved them from the knowledge of greater atrocities

Florence Nightingale, my dear, how I love you:
innocent of the Hiroshima that was to come
you saw it in the stiff Victorian hearts
of the drunken men and uncaring officers
whom you cradled equally in your surrendered arms
amidst the filth and horror of Scutari
where the sodden log-books of history testify beyond romance
that the soldiers kissed your shadow on the wall as you passed
bearing the lamp of all the women who have borne the pain
of masculinity beneath the frilled petticoats of their time
remembered merely as the sweet ladies with the lamps
who sacrificed wealth and marriage for bandages and Christ
casting charitable lights upon the depraved dance
that included them in all its mad reels and steps

I love you, sweet Lady with the Lamp,
and even if you were a man
could you but nurse the dancers out of this sweaty hall
I would dance even with your shadow in this February moonlight

when the last waltz is called
and the last great piper has gone into the hill
I want to arrange a single dance with you
on the polished floor of that empty village hall
with no remaining music but the drumbeat of our hearts
beating like a faint armistice in the long Crimean silence.

In Memory of My Father

That grey patched jersey,
that cap,
those great big hands.

Steam rose from the horses' nostrils,
the silver darling shimmered in the barrel :
flour hay wood nets wool grass sheep brine
Eriskay, Oronsay, Calvay, Mingulay.

What horror stands before me:
memories and this white page.

Shona

And then there was that perpetual moment
as the sun sloped down on the February snow
on a day as crisp as your eyes were to become
as buoyant as your momentous golden hair
as exultant as your lovely laughter
caught ticking on the rolling ground
Ah, my lovely, lovely, lovely darling
my lovely darling crisp and blonde,
your eyes and smile are like a moment
caught momentous in that sun-caught snow.

A Cave In Drumnadrochit

I love you so much
that I could take you
to a cave in Drumnadrochit
where the giant dines with the dragon
on a perpetual feast of chips and red sauce,
red ice cream sauce, ice cream smooth, ice cream cold,
ice cream laughter and ice cream tales
in the green bracken of a croaking world
where human speech is inadequate
to reach the scale of being a frog,
being in love,
petting imaginary scales and teeth
that would consume the world
were they not yours and mine
living in a rural cave
behind a Peter Rabbit door
in a green Highland glen
that's as safe as your cuddle
a genealogical tenderness that abolishes the Clearances
that have left you and I
singing with animal sounds
of the cave to which we would go
in distant Drumnadrochit.

Heaven

The latest magic you've asked for is a carpet
to take you to sweet Arabia beyond the seas
with one corner in your pink bedroom
and the other in Ali Baba's cave
where MacCrimmon has become lost forever
in that land between perfection and the possible
where the great lament goes on and on
veering between the ordinary and the grace note
that speaks of our locked embrace
in Uist where the white sand stretches to infinity
and in that glade where we picked bluebells one day
like an important piobrach which we would never forget
the fragile leaves summoning us to the necessity of a heaven
which we gathered in our aching arms that day for this one day
now made accessible in the constant vase of your magic
and in the perpetually renewed water of my lament :
two great pipe tunes twinning into the one great music.

Someone Else

Someone died in Finland a moment ago
and a child or mother or father grieved
for someone precious as you
complete in my arms this night your skin like snow
and your closed eyes dancing in the light
my eternal darling
was it you I saw in Ballyshannon
with a bullet through your breast
and tears mingling with your blood
and though I have tried to sacrifice you
my dearest love
to the separate carnage of Lockerbie
it is as if I was Abraham forbidden at the knife
to destroy the very thing that separates me
from someone else.

Dedication

And the river sparking like silver
above the Dog Falls
last July as Glen Affric blazed in the summer sun
and we dabbled in the still river
holding hands
for a moment that did not last forever

and I hear that the days are foreordained
in which I love you so much
that I would scoop up that gentle river
from source to mouth
spoon by tiny spoon

and if the days are filled with heroin
and prostitution and drunken nights
I dedicate to you this ordained river
from source to mouth
drop by drop
in full winter spate
and frozen white in early spring
and choked with fallen autumn leaves

that perpetually alters the course and shape
of this red river
that runs in dappled light wherever I go.

This Simple Thing

One foot in Uist
and one foot in Edinburgh
how I seek to alter the world for you
this grave and machair made eloquent
this cobbled street made safe and immortal
this brutality ignored
that house in which I was born restored
savage time and circumstances altered
between Ankara and Askernish
while the inexplicable drives us to tears
that the very simplest thing can not be solved
that I cannot delay this train
cannot stay this day
cannot alter a single thing
O Christ, forgive me how I say that name,
I want to give you cheesecake on the moon
and tell you of the great poetic art and bards
and all I am is this weak and useless thing
this man
who cannot stay this moment
eternalise this kiss
explain this train that goes away
express a thing
O, I believe all right,
I believe in this Christ, this King,
this eternal change that being
born again doth bring
believe me also
when I say I love you
though I cannot change a single circumstance
I love you
in the devilish imbalance of every contrary thing.

Tonight

Tonight you were like fresh rain again

```
          s
        - p
      t     r
    e         a
  j             y
```
gish-gash, ah, ah,

ash on an old man's sleeve is all the ash burnt roses leave

tonight: now there's a night: TONIGHT:

tonight you're mine (completely), ah, ah, jet-spray gish-gash
ash, ash on an old man's sleeve, ash is all the ash burnt roses
leave
tonight

tonight, tonight you were like fresh rain again,
(like rain falling on a mown field)
making stubble wet
corn damp
plop on the sea
mossy rocks GLISTENING
yuck-a, yuck-a, yuck-a, lips

smacking.

When I was young there was a ridge on the machair where the corn
and the barley and the hay were planted each spring. When
summer came we would go down there and, playing amongst the
wild poppies and secret ditches, watch the grown-ups raking,
gathering the harvest, smoking, going home We too would then go
home with our mother, perhaps visiting someone on the way.

Perfection

"When perfection comes, the imperfect disappears". I Corinthians
13:10.

Lest I bind you with perfection
and cripple you with my love
know that it is out of failure
that I see you the clouds in the sky
and when a man walks down the street
you are the image of that man when young
playing stickle-back across the cobbles
when I read a letter written in the war
you wrote it by an oil lamp perhaps in Galloway
where the Irish coast was near in day
I see the waves on Boisdale beach
and, for no reason, San Francisco bridge
comes into my mind and you walking on it
plucking a rose rose in the botanic garden
asking for a coloured straw for your coca-cola
and a vocabulary alight with your excitement
where vowels are coloured balls and rowing boats
speeding across the bonny sea to Skye
or at a changed consonant into a plane, Outer Space, where
the bus, and you reminding me that there are no seat belts,
veers round the fast corners and what is the capital
of the United States, New York, tell me a word beginning with
p poppy, parantula, pipe-band, PacCrimmon's Plament,
pippopotamus,
and do you still scratch your nose when uncertain
that distance is not as measured by your infant eye
where you climb a tree and survey cats and birds
that once vocabularised around our dreams of a sacrament,
Corinthians, that which you once worshipped as unknown

I now proclaim to you as that which you are and yet are not
you are what I know you are though you are not
what I know you are not, you are, you are.

Between October and April

There was a time when our universe was a tree
one winter's length ago   you
playing houses   amidst the mud and branches   hanging
an umbrella in the fir, a paper aeroplane in the highest twig,
the north end a bedroom, the south a kitchen, and swooping doors
where you pleased - sometimes as many as fifteen, sometimes   none

in the foetus, before the doctor's news,
there was a time when my universe was not   you
one winter's length ago   you
curled, a miniature Bahamas, ten shapely fingers, a bumpity-bump
of breath
breath breathing   shapity-shape   shapity-shape   shapity-shape

and now

you wearing   pyjamas, blue mittens, shoes, a dress, blue jeans,
                a wrist-watch, bangles of flowers - let me stop

and

if I could transport myself   between October and April
                                between the roots and the branches
                                between the seed and the flower
                                between not life and not death

        I would declare LOVE, despite Ceacescu
perfected in the whatwasness there is now and now and now and now
and now.

Gerinish

Nothing is distant anymore:
all is Uist, and Constantinople is no more,
my sisters married to Muslims and Jews,
I cannot offer you the rococo poetry of Rome
or the post-modernist experience of America
for I have come home in the expectation of failure,
the certain knowledge that the thatch has gone
and that the gentle road on which my father walked
was the road out of which Germaine Greer emerged
like an airman on the Gerinish machair
signaling that the rocket was ready to be launched
and that afterwards we could play treasure-hunt
and then go home by bus to Boisdale

where I didn't know that the tilley lamp was just that
while an evil witch-hunt went on in America
that is now as far away as Salem
and as near as the new fundamentalist terror
that draws Boisdale next to Belsen

and brings me home, wherever that is,
here at this borrowed typewriter in Edinburgh
where exile and security have become indivisible
drawing us back into the foetus, having taste death,
where no one was foolish or blinded by memory,
content in the caved-in houses, satisfied with the dim rattle of the
TV,
secure in the firstness of things before

The Single Pearl

It is not complete this night
as we sing to one another down the phone
we address the absent portions of the heart
that was removed to the corn prairies of Canada
like that unreachable note that Beethoven sought deaf
the poet Robert Fergusson reduced to eating straw in Bedlam
because of the single pearl that was absent
you
my beloved
making their insanity freshly necessary this very night.

Talk To Me

Talk to me for a long long time
and I will listen to your every word
and though I cannot promise to understand them all
I will retain them in the pyramid of my heart
until that day in which the sun will shine
mathematically into the centre of the targe
which will remove the very stones that will reveal
the ark of our covenant love
emblazoned with Highland gold
my beloved
the glory does not rest in this casket we construct
for heaven itself is the pyramid apex
and the earth, Skye, its footstool
but that haphazard word of yours will adorn the ark
and that tale of mine is emblazoned on the side
and on it is a picture of the mountains of Kintail
and the very sandy shore we talked about last night
our incomplete conversations broken tablets of stone
made perfect by love which this casket can not hold.

Is Your Collar Open?

Turning
in your old shirts,
and the soft movement outside,
the warmth of love,
the final seal.

And in the gloaming
your head and shoulders encased the light
and softly spoke
and softly spoke
and softly spoke.

Baldness and white hair
and a local globe of a face
rivered with the known,
a mountaineous landscape of plenty
an ocean of white waves.

And is your collar open
you would say finally,
is your collar open?

And I choke back the tears
on that final darkness,
the love of old collars,
your tears as you saw us
towards our university days in our old shirts,
in our old shirts of poverty and love
that were fully open,
displayed exposure.

And my collar was open, so open that it could never close again,
opened waiting for your word,
your hair, your face, your light,
and is your collar open,
is your collar open
is your collar open.

Ah yes, it's open, father,
it's open, Dad,
it's open, open, open.

The Magic Clock

Do not ask for coffee
my darling
but take me
to that play area of your heart
where the smooth slide glides
and the wooden trains chug on time
beneath the penguin clock
where we have constantly embraced
waiting for the hour to strike
and the magic doors to open
to reveal
a monkey on a tree
a lamb on a roundabout
and a dolphin flying high

for in the coffee shop
my darling
I stabbed a needle through my arm
and sank into the flames again
on a final day without beginning
that may never end
this hellish separation
that has left a fearful chasm
and a religious bridge
between the innocent and the guilty

the toy shop and the coffee shop
where you play and I sip coffee
until the next hour strikes
and the magic doors open again
to reveal
a monkey on a tree
a lamb on a roundabout
and a dolphin flying high

Do not ask for coffee
my darling
but take me
to that play area of your heart
where the smooth slide glides
and the wooden trains chug on time
beneath the penguin clock
where we have constantly embraced
waiting for the hour to strike
and the magic doors to open
to reveal
a monkey on a tree
a lamb on a roundabout
and a dolphin flying high.

Innocence

As this phone rings again and again
I exonerate you from all blame
because you have not made any of the decisions
that have purged our hearts with pain

and left us absent
from the places we know we'd want to be

if it were possible to be stuck starfish on the shore
inseparable by land or sea
situated in a landscape of our acquaintance
judging a sand-dune to be here,
an ocean wave to be there,

knowing that principle cannot emerge from chaos
I confess how close I am each moment to cracking
from love that would drown for you
to an anger that would swamp you with blame
for being where you have no choice but to be

forgive me that I would consign you to that asylum,
that dry-dock,
for laughing at nothing
except that at which I laugh heartily myself
before the constant tears humble me
when the ordinariness of your life
sweeps over me like a little wave at Nairn

telling me that paranoia
has been altered into a dream
and that when I saw you in your mother's arms
in the quiet hedges of Inverness
you were sailing like an ocean galley
even with the twin heads of Castor and Pollux
through the spray and spindrift into this very epistle.

Some Things Made No Impact

Tonight, talking incidentally of death,
I heard again, for the first time,
and saw the charred ruins of your stone cottage
where grandad and granny and the two children burnt to death
when I was a star and shining high in the solid firmament,
re-making the world, moulding my times, shaping the future
that is now this night and I hearing, not for the first time,
of your death : some things made no impact until tonight.

At My Grandfather's Grave

Eriskay
on a Saturday afternoon
and your name was Angus Campbell
Sorley spoke well of you
how you made a Gael of the Gall
in those round necked jerseys
fishing schools
and my acquaintance Maoileas had just written
how wisdom was different from knowledge
as your name remained
in that place almost known of the Bonnie Prince
where the dry politician sells whisky
and the ferry leaves on time
my darling in a distant country
all this is yours
even though Paul cautioned us
not to be consumed
by endless myths and genealogies
how crucified I felt
as I refused to contemplate the word rape
if there was even hint of my complicity involved
and called it bourgeois robbery
my child
that here I am
bound and gagged
by the very thieves I brought in
(though this is also called the consequence of sin)
while they sell you
the cheap and tawdry trinkets of Inverbervie
stone upon fine stone
school and fine flowers

and my joy my love my child
even though I know
that he who looks back is not worthy to be called
that there really is a place
where thieves cannot break in and steal
though moth and rust decays
that grave where a name stands
and Ben Scridein is as she was
and Mgr Ailean's signature is in the books
and even as I left to see you
the morning sun rose red on blue Ben More
and the still trout lochs were as they were
forgiving all complicity in the declaration of the kingdom
the Gaelic world that is
stating that Angus' death in 1930
was really neither here nor there.

For My Mother

Later on
when I became imperfect myself
I understood you had done your best
though I used to be ashamed of you
smelling of fish-oil and failure
in that deodorised bourgeois world
behind which lay
the equal imperfections of fawning greed
and petty piteous success
where equal mortal tears have flowed
from silver girls who were exalted in my heart
my shame has known no bounds
my love
of the pity of the human condition
where even now I would exalt you in my heart
till you turned to silver or to gold
became a ballerina and a fairy queen
impervious to shame or praise
waltzing at your stumbling best.

Five Children Gunned Down in California

Here there is no uniform,
no generals we can see strutting across fascist yards,
the Annie Jane going down off Vatersay,
the Iolaire sinking off Stornoway,
Patrick Sellar is missing however
though the beautiful green valley is all ablaze
and the cold ruined stances of houses smoulder
in the sweet ashes of the lovely morning light
as it hits the high beauty of Foinavon
and mirrors across the moors of this Mackay country
where I see no military order or Inquisition
or crooked finger calling us to the official front
that besieged the rye grass when I was young
in Uist I remember lying in the Boisdale grass
imagining that Hitler had risen from the dead
and was hiding in the potato fields of Bornish
already for the assault of the night and could I
cut the telegraph wires before he arrived
at the corner of the field at the edge of the house
where his forgotten shadow suddenly startles this night
the five innocent children who have died again
in the indiscriminate Boisdale of the unordered mind.

After the Rain

All of a sudden
the rain stopped.

And I looked out of the window
across the Corstorphine hill
and the Forth Bridge just visible
in the October mist.

And perhaps it was the way –
yes I shall say it –
the grass groaned dairy green in the six o'clock dew
but I remembered a drying moment
when the wet steaming cattle lowed
in those after-school hours
that call you now
to that perpetual rehearsal
can the years be numbered
from age to age
from me to you
that place which I have sought in my own father's eyes
and may have glanced one day in distant Strontian
or seen here in Granton between
the film which rolls and rolls
O how you rise Johnny MacNeil
in the dead of Nova Scotia
an accordion tune of that one brief dance of your past
waving and rising between Hiroshima and Easdale
touching now even now
across where even now the smirr now newly falls again
to Bathgate and Wishaw and Glasgow.

I am here my darling
I am here I scream

I am here to grant you my eyes out of this soft Scots rain
as I wish you there
where I had been
except fulfilled and eternal

stand there my love
in the after rain
that evening of this kiss
before alcohol and rock and roll

stand there my love
in my thatched heart
just drying yourself after the plunging Uist rain
your dark smouldering hair curled like Mingulay
ashes on fire in the green-black stove
your silvery stones dancing in the sudden light

stand there my love
and hold my hand my love my echo my darling
my drying rock after the rain
my mist after the storm
my world after my Uist.

Sibelius

Five years old in South Uist
as you died in Finlandia

such great ignorance is mine
those trees and lakes and snowy landscapes

driving you to the misfortune of music
and the silent addictive acclaim

that laid you beside Mozart and Beethoven
and Hadyn and the great Tchaichovsky

consigned to the romantic safety of ancient history
that classic distant rapture

that weaves across those northern landscapes
to that uncertain child in Boisdale and Garrynamonie

kicking stones with his wellies
and fetching water from the frozen well

and battling for the crust of bread
that drove you to compose unknown for me.

No Turning Back

Those university days
are as ancient now
as going down to Oxford
in those strange stiff uniforms
that were not like our
fancy flares and beads and denim shirts
which none of us have taken off
and which have chained us
to the terrible territory of a yesterday
which even as it promised me its Joni Mitchell looks
suddenly vanished
only to taunt and haunt me for twenty years
through the sought hell of drink
which has finally delivered me
into this soft July evening in Edinburgh
conscious of today's great pain and tears
but needing to prefer them
to the vain promises of the long dead corpse
which even now in my fallen human folly
I would, were it left to me,
irrationally resurrect into the dawn
that already has the promise that is not vain.

Jane

And despite it all
what I remember
are your red red lips at twenty
and the morning tide of our love
racing through the Highland glens
before the morning broke and the sirens rang
and the human frailty
that even this poem demonstrates
removed us from Church Street to Armageddon,
to an age where grace was received
that expunged the cells and shame
that had stilled your lovely smile
so that through this cloudy windy day
in distant beautiful Edinburgh
I can clearly see you
as you were that night
red-mouthed and beautiful
with a smile which circumstances can not erase,
for you see her smiling there that lovely smile each distant day.

Remembering Davie Welsh

These were no iced east winds
that knived us
but I cast the colour aside
for the pint in the fat barrel
that grieved you
until you died,
and it was only this morning
that the dungareed image of God
was seen in the spewed street in which I live
sawing wood, sawing wood.

There was a river
which made glad your heart
as you heard my poetry and my promise
before the terrible iced east wind days
were released around them,
forming those early icicles
even as we shared our dreams.

And even as they were forming
they were melting
as you died in the interval
between creation and renewal
and while the iced east winds are slackening
we somehow stand there
with a beer or two that may even have been innocent
shouldering a joyous armistice
which had never conceived the trenches
which were a step on either side.

Human Rights

"I obeyed orders and followed the crowd ....
all of it was a mistake": A former Nazi.

Here, for starters, are some of those who've brought it on themselves:
homosexuals, prostitutes, some of the unemployed, Jews and crofters -
all those who, if given the proverbial inch, will take more than a mile:
loungers and spongers and parasites, leeches and freeches and screeches,
Auchwitz, Strathnaver, Africa : wherever there is a crowd,
smoke burning, acrid flesh black, and the word reverberating

Thatcher, Thatcher, Thatcher, Thatcher : not you Margaret,
but you, Thatcher made remote made flesh
goose-stepping Hitler with that ridiculous moustache -
how was that possible?

Goose-stepping Hitler with that ridiculous moustache
and a whole nation, a whole nation, saluting:
in Uist John Gordon of Cluny was the landlord,
in Lewis the opium-king Matheson,
ridiculous moustaches and starvation,
ridiculous moustaches and the gas chambers.

Here, for instance, is a list of powerful people :
Genghis Khan, Napoleon, the Duchess of Sutherland, Mussolini.
And here, for instance, is a list of Highlanders :
Donald John MacAskill, Iain MacIsaac, Neil Campbell.
The graveyards are full.

In my own instance, for example, this is what I felt and wrote :

I.
How is it that we have grown so far apart
that our languages are incomprehensible,
the crofter and the countess
as far apart as hate is from love :
I do not understand your sherry cabinets
any more than you understand my Gaelic verbs
in this reluctant Ross-shire evening
I remember when I led your droves to Falkirk
and how you delighted in the tales of the raids,
whether mythical or not,
and I remember one morning you walked to my cottage
and drank the milk warm from the cow's udder
and invited me up to a reception you were holding that evening
before our languages became distant and foreign,
further apart than even death itself.

II.
It is all exile
now that the severance has come
whether it be Canada, Glasgow, or Uist,
you have taken from me all that was mine
and given me the wine bitter with gall
that I was the cause of my own misfortune
by foolishly losing at Culloden
and then bringing children and poverty to the glen
so that nothing but arithmetic eviction remained
as the single solution for you in your glass castle
where you view surplus emotion through each opaque wall
as a regrettable hindrance to your plan and conscience

God knows that if brochures were available
I would have received the full glossy ones
advertising the corn prairies of Canada
and the promised land of Govan
opening their doors to heroes made useful
by the certification of clanship and trust
who died for their land and chief
even when they knew that betrayal was in the air

I heard you on the phone last night
telling me that, in the circumstances,
exile was the best solution,
and that Canada offered great prospects for a man like me
who could read poetry in Toronto and Montreal
and travel on those great lakes in summer days
clear of the debilitating poverty of the glens
and the battles that had destroyed our friends:
you almost convinced me, in fact, that my own death would be
useful,
that even Glasgow with all its declensions
was an appropriate environment for an alcoholic poet
to become a phoenix, even if it was only a Highland phoenix.

III.
There was a time when I wanted to go to sea
sailing as an officer across the world's geography
Empire maps that were red and green
a time even when, though admittedly at a pinch,
the Royal Navy or the Marines would have done.

I see them at Fort George strutting across the concrete,
exiles from Carinish heading for Ypres:
Lads, March at Ease.

IV.

How can I acknowledge that you are dying tonight
when I see you dancing in the Plaza Ballroom
after the sirens and the distress had died away
and the Highlanders gathered like herons on the shore
cackling round Rubha na h-Ordaig on an April day,
coats muffled against the breeze, mother,
the tram cars trundle through the city
to the photograph you saw tonight, my darling,
of me painting the house the year before you were born.

V.

When I look up
now, the blueness of the night again,
I still see you at the castle window
on the edge of jumping
do not let that brutal bitterness do it
my love
stand at that incomprehensible curtain
looking at the glens of Ross-shire
turning white under your command
at your word they turn red and green and blue,
a rainbow, Countess, a loch in Uist,
o God, if it has to be, even that kiss on the butterfly farm.

VI.

This is the great wonder, surely, Thatcher,
that you know what is best for me:
there is a ship sailing to Canada next week
and if you are not on it, let's say willingly,
I will send the factor round with a summons
which will ignite a thousand cottages inside your heart:
convince yourself that you will miss a great deal
by not sailing to that land that I have made necessary:
call it a cruise, if it pleases you.

VII.

Incidentally, here's a bit of journalism for you:
Donald MacLeod's "Gloomy Memories", by the way -
in case they will influence you - are unbalanced:
not seeing the full economic picture
that necessitated the burning of cottages,
not demonstrating the stubborn reluctance
of those stupid Highlanders
to leave their stables for the acres across the seas
that offered them space and freedom,
they concentrate on the unnecessary suffering
these people brought upon themselves by their own
pigheadedness:
now that you have read this press release
I trust that you will be more sensible.

VIII.

The certificate came through the post today
only requiring the signature of acceptance
that stares at me from Strathnaver and Kildonan
and Dachau and Belsen and Warsaw and Prague
signing on the dotted line of the lesser evil
I confess to having the pen again in my raised hand:
it is no wonder that Purgatory was invented.

IX.

I believe that you are truly honest in your hatred
clearing the glens of the untidy remnants of your people
so that not a hearth or stone or surname will remain
to haunt you with the human cry of our folly
where no ghetto remains
even to cast pity upon the perfidious Jew
who died with all the gracious Macs of my people.

I even believe that you do not truly understand
how it is I just cannot rise and go
with a song in my heart and my bunnet in the air
like a well-paid extra in Brigadoon by the sea.

Go, I hear you say, and make a fresh start:
you are a Highland Warrior
and I can even give you a reference if you wish;
there are vacancies in the factories of Detroit,
Manhattan is crying out for poets,
there may even be vacancies for fruit pickers in California:

seeing you so willingly drank the wine
here are some grapes of wrath for you to deal with:
learn English if you can,
live in the homelands,
sign on if need be,
though I'm sure that the God of your fathers will provide for you.

Whatever you do, bless you.

X.
Sweet sweet countess,
I watched you again standing by your laced window this morning
amazed at the complexity of it all:
looking down you almost asked me why
I wanted to remain in this poverty-stricken glen
with nothing but the bare hills and my dun cow

It is not possible for you to understand
that I do not want your gowns or your castle
your Aryan perfection
or the goldmines that split the Transvaal
any more than it is possible for me to understand
that you do not want my bread and my warm milk
my poetic uncertainty
or the dances that make an Autumn worthwhile

Is it possible for either of us to understand
that what I want are the very stones
and those blades of grass I crushed with my bare feet
as I walked from Culloden for you into the burning glens
and the river and the trees and the byre and the sky
and the smell of kosher food in the backstreets of Casablanca
and the whooping sounds we made as we danced in Edinburgh
and again the river and the trees and the byre and the sky
and anything that would reassure us
that everything is not an eternal void
for me and you.

PS

I love you.

My Husband and I

He sits there like a fallen angel
DOING MY HEAD RIGHT IN

whistling when he wakens
as if our marriage wasn't re-cycled paper, bits of the Express and
Star.

This morning was a particularly bad (or, for me, good) morning.
I don't know if you've ever looked really closely at things, say
things like your pillow when your lying there thinking how really
miserable life is.

Anyway, it was like one huge feather, like a snowy glacier I once
saw in a film, where you fall 3000 feet and not die.

It struck me right then that I was a woman,
that I saw things completely differently from him pulling on his
socks and whistling.
So I laughed, really laughed. Right out loud.

He asked me what was wrong with me and, of course, I said
"Nothing", as at the very beginning.

Mallaig

Five a.m.
and what noises of grace
emerge from this council estate:
birds singing on the TV aerials
and a car door slamming shut

this is Mallaig on an August morning
when I was a young reporter and thrilled
by the seagulls squawking in the herring light
and the shop doors opening
to the warm smells of pies and coffee
when I used to drive across the Highland moors
and pull in by the early afternoon
to view the eagles swooping down
upon the grazing sheep above Loch Hourn

and each night I would phone you
from the red kiosk beside the loch
and tell you that I loved you
and that we would never part from Mallaig,
a gracious memory on this strange Edinburgh morning.

For Sorley MacLean

Now that this great century is drawing to its close
what remains
after Nagasaki and the school closures
are your marvellous words
astonishing as the Cuillins
Preshal in early May
Blaven on the near horizon
Sarajevo on that distant day
when the trenches took five million
and Stalin another ten
the brute and brigand
Hiroshoma and Nagasaki
Korea and Vietnam
Ulster and Iran
thirty, forty, or maybe fifty million
leaping in the face or horror
while your song and serene music
made imperishable the sore frailty of this lasting cause
for art has spoken
Deirdre of the thousand tears has cried,
Cu-chumhail has stepped out with his hounds,
Eimhir has revealed her gold yellow hair,
and though the great and good have gone
with the mean-spirited and the indifferent
the world is still beautiful
in the great company of your generous poetry
where they remain
because their mouths were red and proud with the old song
which you recognised even in me those eighteen years ago
and which neither folly nor prostitution has destroyed
for the girl of the gold yellow hair still lives

beyond the spite of the bourgeoisie
and the feebleness of our dismal Scotland
the dust is not weak
for your heart is the heart of your people
your art is the art of the Gael
the song of Uist,
the great music of Kintail,
words that stopped time, the deer,
not only in the fruitful wood of Hallaig
but in the budding birch trees of our minds
where the lovely congregation of the girls, your songs, still sing.

Scotland

The ease with which her dress slipped off
astonished me even more than our subsequent failure
to make love in those Glasgow evenings
when all was cotton dresses and a form of youth
brought up on the dreams of the perfection of a kiss
and the possibility of a cottage in Argyll:

later on you wrote to me
as air hostess in Surrey
and I where I was not where I was
that Saturday morning I preferred a football match to you
during the game seeing the print upon your swirling dress
and the way your hair bounced and your breasts small in August
when time had not yet crossed into that perfect X
that dispatched its favour to those hurt far less
by the knowledge that our love was not true
but a desire for love, just love itself,
the shadow of a cheekbone, the slim turn of a thigh, a Glasgow thought,
and the question hard and not worthy of what we felt

where the skies roar
nothing now restricts our independence
but that same virginity that protected the hope
that something really was precious beyond the sudden vote.

On Summer Nights

On summer nights
he would walk the cockle strand
out of history
black-bereted and striding
across the vast ridged sand
until one day he put on his uniform
and saluted the sun in the sky
and ran off to the sea
that he'd left before I was born
and later on I heard he'd died.

Sometimes on summer nights
I don my full buttoned uniform
and walk the bridge
of lager lights
and malt cliffs
that shimmer past in Atlantic neon lights
waiting for my equal madness
from the black-beret of the cockle strand
to the glittering uniform that is my equal end.

On Boisdale Machair

How happy they seemed with their portion
in the land of the living
in those August days
smelling sweetly of wild poppies and paraffin
amidst the rigs o' barley and long golden corn
before I died
and saw them moving still
in smoked satisfaction
amidst the ricks of hay and stubble
that was their Autumn fruit
pomegranate red
in the unimagined bowl that was an urn
while elsewhere in the controlled lamplight
downed with light brown hair
they also clenched the rope
that never held
but held the time, their time,
mine that has vanished in the last half hour
and though the hay was in
years before my death
you daily died in unshed tears
bruised before that flashing August came
and perhaps I spilt them for you dear, my dear,
and as I finished speaking I almost spilt some more
my child
for the ones you will spill for me for you
for me for you
beyond that August day
beyond the hay
I smile, I laugh, I love you
even though you may -
oh, you may, you may, you may.

Pot of Soup

I made a pot of soup on Christmas Eve
and knew that you would have been proud of me
as the carrots and turnips became whelks and herring
that swam and swelled and took on form
that swallowed up the infirmity
that lay out there in the darkness
in the deafness that beset me when I was young
on that prodigal path I took from your mighty arms

I slide my degrees and career success
into this bubbling broth of a Highland soup
simmering with a beautiful fragrance
that would overcome the winter snow
and all the poetry of Eliot and Frost
and all the instant meals I know.

The Gaelic Language

Is an old boxer, flabby, remembering victories.

The greatest, without doubt, was Muhammed Ali
once floating like a butterfly and stinging like
the great pain in his moon eyes mumbling
oh Manila nights, Louisville on the lovely lips,
Buddy Holly cracking like a fresh wireless,

men telling tales, the women at the washing,

the butterflies and the bees.

One Day He Walked Strong About The Hills

There was a one-armed drunken man
who lived alone
in a derelict cottage
with nothing
but a ewe lamb
and how he'd reached that state I neither know nor care
and one day
he tried to wave to you
but you thought it was
animosity
so I saw you go in
and cut off his other arm in thin
red slices that screamed forever
until they reached Cordale bay and were maybe drowned
and next time I saw him
he said he felt no pain
and had been that way since he was born
but neither that lie
nor all the love poems in the whole world
can wash away his agony
as you wave to him from your car
and how he hates himself
for he always waves back and smiles
and it is now neither seen as
love or animosity
but only a meaningless shift of the shoulders
that only the lamb perceives or understands.

My Future Mother-In-Law in Strathnairn In The Fifties

There were one or two vulnerable occasions,
when the great fire roared in the front lounge
and the coffee, or perhaps a dram, was poured
and you talked to me about what was decent and gentle:
how you were once impetuous
and would suddenly jump into the old Austin, and go off to pick
berries,
pushing out the window and letting the collied air in,
the whiff of heather, the bleating of sheep, country matters.

Very probably - though this is my idea -
you sang as you drove along
and your young children, my wife, charmed in the back by the red
leather
and the absolute swiftness of the bracken country travelling by.

I remind myself that the fifties were universal:
Uist was not the only place for aprons and black perms,
chickens also in your strawed yard, and dung and potatoes and
lace
and the same BBC playing that rural light music.

When divorce comes
I suppose that geography goes along with everything else:
the glens bitter, the wind in the windowed air imagined, the
uselessness.

I see them, I who never saw them, permanently in the glen:
they are there transfixed by time,
the old black Austin driving through Strathnairn,
the fragrance of the fragrant leather,
the ripeness of the black berries
and you - very probably - singing as you drove along.

Here seems a much more compact time,
as if a soldier, returning from the 1st World War, had dreamed
and believed no-one any more,
least of all a young soldier talking of green fields and victory.

And history,
though there were one or two vulnerable occasions
when the great fire roared in the front lounge etcetera,
has, I suppose, proved him right.

Occasionally, when this typewriter types what's almost right,
I remember you with love, even with affection
for how we have both lost the great moments,
the old black cars by the white streams, the working collies
barking,
the excitement of sailing, singing "Tipperary", to France,
Strathnairn permanent in bracken green and brown,
the old Austin, the red berries, the red leather, Uist
and the holy music without interruption.

Do Unto Others

Mercy triumphs over judgement

as they nailed you to a tree
for claiming to be

the Son of God

and when I was naked you clothed me
when hungry did you feed me
when thirsty did you give me to drink
when in prison did you visit me
when I was sick did you comfort me

with unrequited love
did I in any way meet the vows
that I would love you until you died

with that believed love
that does not envy or boast
with that sought love
that bears no record of wrongs

even as you evict me, penniless,
from the blazing cottage which you own
and we huddle in that pathetic graveyard at Croick
while the big party goes on up in the Big House

and I hear the minister tinkling the sherry
and a balloon being burst
and the sound of laughter
mixes with the children's cries
and hear you saying that it served them right
for being a wicked generation

I willingly join them in scrawling my name
in that available window
in an effort at scratching
sense out of horror

knowing that at whatever point you judge another
I condemn myself

and when you were homeless did I house you
and when you were hungry did I feed you

son of a carpenter
son of a carpenter
bruised for our transgressions
crushed for our iniquities
you have been marginalised
like the useless cottar
and my ageing mother

seeking the love
that would extinguish
the terrible holocaust of our selfish hearts.

Spastics' Bus

As it passed me, slowly,
our faces locked for a moment
and then one in the back, a girl I think,
smiled and waved
and I hesitated thinking they were mocking me
until I smiled and waved back
and suddenly it was an ocean of waves
as the bus turned right,
Thatcher's cabinet going home for tea
prepared by those who asked what they saw that day,
the Dow Jones index, wars and rumours of wars,
me coming home with a fresh batch of paper for my poems,
a bearded man waved at us in April
plastic cups that cannot spill for Douglas Hurd
the consolation of love, an embrace, here at 5pm
and then television, and bed.

Salvation

"I am ashamed now to confess that I trembled more before the factor than before the Lord of Lords".
Donald MacAskill, Highland Land Reform Meeting 1884.

The theology is to be found in the first chapter of Romans:
there we boldly, and in faith,
declare that I am not ashamed of the gospel
for it is the power of God unto salvation,
I hear you cry, Donald, in the confession of the machair,
and in the epistle of the shore, in the psalm of the moor,
in the covenant of your birth, in the circumcision of your house,
in the atonement of your closaid, in the redemption of your byre,
in the resurrection of your barley, in the chorus of your field,
in the name that once passed your lips
that all is changed, changed utterly.
that a terrible beauty is born again
in the accusation of your shame I see your starving mother
and your starving children, and your starving children's starving
children
sharing the fear that has adorned my gospel
where the factor is no more than a clerk in a golf club office
and Tokyo is as near to Boisdale as eviction was to your poverty

my God, where would this poor man rest his head
but on the bare rocks swept by snow and storm
and the potatoes raw before the fine legal words
that at a nod would consign him to the sea's edge
where my trembling heart, Donald can I claim your name,
proclaims that your eternal Christ saved the afflicted
as they were whipped into the great grey storms
that left the equal wreckage of broken barns and crystal glasses
as if it had all been terribly accidental, like an equinoxal gale,

my wife out there slipping on the stranded rocks
where the tied seaweed lashes the tied moss
and Christ on the headland, Donald, whether we drown or not.

No Explanations

Thirty candles glowing
in vast expectation
as she stood beside me
taller than big Jean Brodie
waiting for the explanation
that would extinguish the difference
between English and Gaelic,
the confusion of race and identity,
and oh that I would have known
of Columba and Alasdair MacColla
or screamed of the MacMhuirichs
or gone on my knees to say "2 Corinthians 5",
but all I knew
was that my Gaelic father was only a joiner
and that my Gaelic mother scrubbed floors
in a polished English world
which neither this poem
nor twenty years of time
have extinguished from my Christian mind.

Pliny

They were different
these children
sons of ministers and lawyers
doctors' daughters
in embroidered cotton
strutting across the sixties
into white-heat colleges
that are now as rusty red as UCS
where passion has been dismantled
and the last no-doubt divorced
bolt
rolls down the corridor
where once I glanced upon your rising breasts
made chalky white and pointed
with the sharp Latin of our day.

Another Accolade for Hugh MacDiarmaid, now that he's dead

Aye, it's no go for the merry-go-round, it's no go the rickshaw,
it's no go the puddings and pies, it's no go the speeches:
Slainte, as they say, is it in the Highlands?

Langholm, Langholm,
where have you been?

     I've been to   London
      to visit the   Queen.

Scots, Scots, wha hae, Scots wha hae wi, Scots wha hae wi
MacDiarmid dead,
Scots wham words have often led
WELCOME (meaning FAILTE, as in CEUD MILE)
to the ball:
My lords, ladies and gentlemen, a toast - the late, great Hugh MacDiarmid.

   I have seen them at close of day

   Bring forth the horse, the horse was brought

   I've heard them a-lilting at the ewe-milking

   Suddenly, everyone burst out singing

   The curfew tolls the knell of parting day

Lines like razors   disposable
Lines like pennies   loose change
Lines like smarties   colourful
Lines like   Have you read MacDiarmid?

particularly now that he's dead.

Revelation

How we turn to the streets of gold
where tears are no more
and the alabaster and onyx shining
after the fearful horses have gone
and the seven angels and the seven cups
have consumed the beast and the dragon
forever burning in the lake of fire
while the redeemed of the Lord
sing a new song of glorious triumph

John on an island alone
Stephen being stoned
Elijah hiding in a cave
David on his knees
Moses fleeing to a far country
James pierced with a sword
Christ himself a curse on a tree

and then the vision and the great glory
the storehouse full and the famine avoided
Goliath falling and the holy fire of Pentecost
and the Ascension and the testimony and the persecution
John on an island alone
John on an island alone
John on an island alone
singing Holy Holy Holy
is the Lord God Almighty
Worthy is the Lamb, seated on the throne,
Worthy is the Lamb, who was slain
to receive power and glory and honour and riches
and the name Jesus
John on an island alone
singing to the Lamb alone.

Suitcase

Of the old order,
I like to think that nothing is left
but this, bridge
that a man called Ron Malcolmson
gave me when I left the Highlands
and Edinburgh was a bridge on the horizon
where three shirts and I can't remember
if there was even a picture of you
was encased in a place of stairs
where each had his holdall and his bed
and someone left every second day
to return different to where they'd been
once with catalogued suitcases that would take them
to London (Tower Bridge), or Portugal (The Algarve), or Spain
(Malaga)
where that oddly shaped suitcase lies
once brought perhaps by a man from Kyle
taken by ambulance across the Highland fields
to be changed or to die or to
return different to where he'd been.

Clava Bridge carrying miniature tankers of milk and oil
and your presents bought, then wrapped in green and pink
like an Aladdin's cave erupting the green and the red
yachts flying over the bridge, a plane swinging over the horizon,
Inverness, Tierra del Fuego, the first poem returning and returning,
I write it, I write it, I write it,
for you an old suitcase, korky dale.

Alcoholism

I could titillate you
with tales of drunkenness
or startle you
with sorry tales of my addiction
but they matter not
though they are truth eroded
truth askew

I have spent nights in cells
and drunk the morning scraps
and yet death was neither in the deed
nor in the consequence
but in the birth,
the deception of what was and is,
the human gap between my heart and mind,
the conflict between love and desire.

It was no bed in the bush
or stars I saw, or bread I broke in the river
but suicidal shame that I had failed again
and again
and had truly become
that which we all feared
beneath the gloss and sheen.

Tell us of the poetry, Angus,
of urinating and falling in public places,
bawling ballads of confusion,
sonnets of anger,
elegies of guilt and shame.

Though I compose my own elegy
perhaps you can all write the music
in that eternal effort at unity,
for there was an early evening
when we danced,
you in green and I in grey,
before that morning
when you admitted that what I was
was what I'd been
though you'd tried to see me as you thought I'd seemed
and knew that it had never been
but all was this
and this was this unseemly dreadful thing,
this drink, this song, this love, this sin,
this life where Christ has now stepped in.

Sobriety

The worst time is dazed
when it is not dark, not yet quite light
and reaching out you sense the memory of the half-can
the spilt bottle beneath the bed and dawn somewhere
which will never pass two o'clock
and the thing half-said perhaps half-done
to the perfect idea that became frayed
as the blackout began around 7pm
and then you focus and the wall is there cream
and three pictures, each with trees and a loch
and there's the sideboard neat with your beautiful picture in the
centre
and the curtains are drawn and the green clock ticks and cat purrs
at the door where my dressing gown hangs
waiting for that slippered walk into the kitchen
and the fresh milk poured and the toast and the marmalade
and the order that I once dismissed as bourgeois
balm in Gilead, the dew on Mount Hermon,
and the possibility of the postman bringing
the image of your face the reflection of your smile
rain wind and snow outside and April breaking forth
a man walking on the grass, a lorry turning in the yard,
even the pigeon cooing in the single tree
and the certain knowledge, finally,
that I will get through this day
though the earth itself give way
and yes the mountains, yes the mountains themselves
fall into the very heart of the very deep sea.

Kay Matheson

If I could shed a thousand tears
to restore your youth I would shed a million
that your Jerusalem has fallen to the infidels
who will tarnish your name with nothing better than innuendo
I remember you even when I didn't know you
as the young girl who offered radical hope
that the future offered more than Thatcherism
in Uist they tell me you used to cycle miles
through the machair villages to the homes you knew
offered a medieval landscape to your vibrant mind
that faith and hope and what was then called charity
had a place which neither English nor colonialism could displace
before the people's insipid hearts turned their backs on you
and you retreated to the Gairloch of your infant days
where the huge open wind whipped across Loch Broom
and the thin Ballachullish slates tore off the houses
made genteel by the English landlords whom you despised
for the inevitable destruction of their class and arrogance
the fiery arrows of the poison of the failure of your own
turning to TV and the sly ways of the English
those distant machair homes sinking into the Penenirine sand
where nothing remains but the great white spirit of Russia
and, even as I write this elegy, my daughter in a new world,
and the sudden rising of a light wind of anger off Scone.

The Golden Calf

It is neither the sound of victory
nor the sound of defeat that I hear
but the sound of singing
ringing round the camp-fire of indifference
where the gold just happened to turn into a calf

down Lothian Road there is singing in my ears
in those sacramental tents
where communion is all things to all men
I yield my commandments to the priestess of the bar
whose startling cocktails are insufficient
to restore the unbroken covenant of the broken stone

and him telling me later with a radiant smile
that he loved me even more than Mount Sinai
as I held his arms up into the burning sky
crystal blue with the essential grace of our idolatry.

On Reading Wole Soyinka

At last, here is poetry that is necessary:
the pain of Africa and the sloth of the west
crying out, like Abel's blood from the ground,
the very stones themselves crying out,
words without which Africa would be less than black,
without which America would rub the full stomach of its obesity,
the cry echoing out that all, all, is vanity:

I fear to speak of you Africa
lost somewhere between the Empire maps of my childhood
and the political atrocities that our living rooms now share
for fear that my words would be tarnished with Botha's white vocabulary
and the cheap talk of studio and page
or even the familiar retreat into my own slavish history
to discover a Gaelic that Botha would not understand
even though he were to torture us with an absence of poetry
and threaten me with excommunication for pagan dealings

there are those who light fires on remote islands
glorying in the dawning of the dawn and in dusk's falling
remember ancient runes and chants that the God of Mingulay
looks down with mercy on the Countess as well as the cottar
trying to be human in this savage world

armed police crush heads
that starve because I voted for Thatcher
and watched her lisp Christian platitudes to the naked dead
who forgave her as we too have been forgiven
you brood of vipers who strain a gnat but swallow a camel
you give a neat tenth of your apartheid spices

but neglect the more important matters of the law
that is no longer a law but my promise
that justice and mercy and faithfulness
are lost souls which your white hearts exclude
with the incredible profanity of my attached name

all I see are curled heads,
the dishonour of tradition,
and a staff striking against the hard rock
out of which gushes little more than self-justification and image,
Blondin catapulting over the falls,
Samuel Johnson dining with the lord,
every image but the image of God,

made flesh in Soweto
with the dignity of St Kilda
where my own black people were massacred
by religious joylessness and isolation
before the mail boats took them into the homelands
of televised Johannesburg and the liberty of Manhattan
to die a death as brutal as starvation or a cliff-fall,
the reward of a television interview replacing the fat gannet
that may have made the necessary precipice worthwhile

Africa
where a Nigerian Sorley chisels words high as the Cuillin
pagan peaks hit the sky
with an impact more godly than crystal cathedrals
where Dan Quayle means equally well
with opposing words that now have no human status
beyond the dual blindness of our black and white vision.

Brothers in Arms

Were it not for Freud
and our half-knowledge
I might not have been so hurt
when you treated me as a slave and child
after our father died
and love withdrew
and compassion was no more
but selfish pride which fed and fired
those blurred brutal roles we played
slaves to the void
which sucked us into the black haphazard holes
of your dominion and my hatred
(or was it the other way round)
and dropped us scarred
into the chaotic universe of yesterday
which casts its drunken Gaelic television shadow
even on this redeemed and exiled day
in which I still expect to be patronised
and in which you still expect to be rejected
one for art
one for honesty
O Cain and Abel, Esau and Jacob, Joseph and your brothers
I think I know the choice
that separates
preserve us from our unyielding certainties
from lack of love
unforgiveness
from dreams as much as blemishes
even within this perfected world where now I dwell
where Christ
and Christ alone

can wholly heal
the universal Freudian consequences
of that ancient pain
called sin.

The Greatest Gift

"Hearts are not had as a gift, but hearts are earned by those that
are not entirely beautiful": W.B. Yeats.

I saw a cripple today, a boy of twelve
and him playing football with the others,
the ball sailing, floating, pirouetting, if
I kicked it hard enough it would reach Spain,
and bounce on to Rosemarkie and across to Iceland
and down to Canada where my emigrant sister would hold it for a
moment
before flinging it across the ocean, the Pacific or the Minch,
and it would be played in Pakistan and rolled in India
and thrown in China and headed in Poland before
the Pope gathered it in his white vestments
and it became a dove, or perhaps a white rabbit
that I might call Ignatius IV or maybe Calvin
if it was a short-haired one and looked vaguely Presbyterian
whose redeemed heart would earn the lettuce that I would gift him:
I would turn Uist into a giant lettuce,
the airport at Balivanich would become a hutch
and London erased to make a free range for him
to run lovely and white across the Wiltshire Downs
delighting that it had been kicked was now a rabbit
fluffy white, gifted a heart not earned yet earned
because he was, of course, not an entirely beautiful rabbit
but only a poor football of a thing that had given joy to a cripple
whose gift was the white rabbit, the perfect theology of Yeats,
the heart that no one jeered when the game was on and all was possible.

It's Cold On The Lakes

A walking stick.   A plate of potatoes.

                                                                    A log cabin.

Bins

I did not see the incident
but Charlie told me about it, and I trust him:
I also know the tramp, red-bearded in Queen Street station
who forages amidst the refuse like a last dancer.

Anyway, this is the story:
scrambling amidst the bins
he has perhaps forgotten what silver service means
and his mother, or at least his aunt, dandling him on her knees.

One night, let's say it was last year,
Charlie watched him scrachling in the black rubbish
where nothing remained but empty cartons and torn tickets
and the usual poetic symbols that I could include ad infinitum.

So Charlie, let's for the moment say Charlie Malone, recovered alcoholic,
perhaps remembering his own time amidst the bins
bought two fresh sandwiches for him
and simply handed them to him.

And he looked,
first through Charlie, then through the sandwiches,
and flung them on top of the tea dispensary
and returned to foraging amidst the empty bins.

I want to write a great poem here
flowing with eternal symbols, and not just the obvious ones:
poverty, degradation, deprivation, people scrambling amongst the
bins,
but all that rages through my heart is political anger:
ten years of Thatcherism
have left us all scrambling in the scraps,
unable to recognise bread unless it's at the bottom of a bin.

Desert Island Disc

A day without seeing you
and the Pacific starts
up there, in the corner of the room
at first a small wave
trickling down the wallpaper
then an open bay across the bed
and an ocean, a storm, across the floor
and your face not seen in the picture that is not here
and your voice not heard your laugh not imagined
the tips of my fingers touching your forehead
and your cheeks as smooth and soft as this typewriter
where I gaze inside the fifty-one keys to see something,
your name perhaps, or a half-glimpse of your smile
down there where the qwertyuiopasdfghjklzxcvbnm
look up at me like a child asking what's next:
a rest, one hand to my forehead, and the other, five fingers
on the table curled and sort of pointing south-west
and these one hundred and forty words I have just written
smiling back at me and also sort of asking what's next:
another pause, and outside I can hear someone say
"I can see your dirty bum", and a child laughs as
three lights are lit in the flats across the way
where I now see your face again, already in this small page,
after now two hundred and four words your face is in the ribbon
and your mind whirls across the keys as I hit the peddle
and right there, where it says Olivetti, I see your name
and the screw is your eye and q your hair and w your nose
and e your face and r your toe and y your smile and u your teeth
and i your clothes and o your so beautiful where I see you now
swinging on the curtains across the walls stuck to the window panes

and lying on the floor jumping on the bed and twanging my fingers
like a harp outside the boughs of the trees and just everything
including this, the poem that I began to write for you
before I got caught up in this sudden tropical tempest:

Desert Island Disc

On this desert island there is one tree
and I climb it every day
to see if you are coming on a raft across the sea

And there is one small loch
and I dive into it every day
to see if you are amongst the mermaids on the rocks

And there is one solitary stretch of sand
and I search it every day
to see if you've been swimming near at hand

And there is one book (apart from the Bible and Shakespeare)
and I read it every day
to make sure that you still love me before The End.

and here comes that hurricane again
as the Pacific starts
up there, in the corner of the room,
at first a small wave
trickling down the wallpaper
then the stripes on the bed are your coral eyes
and the cupboard hinges lovely words that you once spoke
and each scratch your mark every print your thumb your ankle
turning in this April evening, the sky still and you sleeping
and the absolute silence of the typewriter now,
or at least in a few words time,

every volcanic word you, and the silence you,
and the whiteness from Honolulu to the Bahamas stretching
beginning, in this particular instance, with the word A
and not ever ceasing, in any given instance,
even with the supposedly dumb empty whiteness
that is supposed to cease after the stop after the word You.

Tak a Cup O Kindness Yet

If you look west
my darling
you can see the ruined castle
of Ormiclate
where Clanranald gave the great feasts
and look there
that's where the sixteen-oared galleys sailed to Duntulm
and do you see this remarkable inscription
the original I think
is in the High Museum of Ireland
and one day
my darling
I walked along this piece of shoreline
while Sorley recalled that he had walked with his intelligence
and Yeats' grave you should go there
it speaks of you and me
and I desire
let me think carefully about this my darling
that you will know Picasso
and Dante
and the Book of the Dean of Lismore
and lie on this very knoll
where once I saw the clouds dance in the Highland sky
and whistled music akin to Greensleeves
and even as I talk do you remember
the shoemaker's shop
and the day we sat on his step
eating ice-cream till it melted on our knees
oh my love paint the world like Michelangelo
and dance like Fred Astaire
compose like Mairi Mhòr

and know the MacMhuirichs
and Rob Donn and Uilleam Ros
and the Great Burns
drunk and dead before 36
and his love like a red red rose
know Burns my love
great sinner though he was
looking west and pleading
that we should tak a cup o kindness yet
before we tak the rose.

This Too Shall Pass

Do not be embittered
my love
that the surge of the Atlantic has gone
here on this drive inland

sit back my child
in this green bus seat
and watch the calm country unfold
its foreign charm

Duntelchaig rippling in the breeze
smoke rising from Inverfarigaig chimneys
settled farms and sheep folds
that manifest the ordered journal of Invernesshire

we settled in to our journey
and the crusty driver and the shepherd
become our haphazard companions
as we drift across the still moorland

where we might imagine the Atlantic roar again
and the great wind shipping across Orosay strand
and the corner of your beautiful mouth unzips a smile
that unleashes an Atlantic Ocean on to the parched Hebridean sand.

Speaking To Me Of Culloden

What ecstasy fills my heart this night
that you have spoken to me of Culloden
as you speak of Cinderella and the golden goose,
what ecstasy fills my heart this night
that you have spoken to me of Culloden
as real as Red Riding Hood and the savage wolf,
what ecstasy fills my heart this night
that you have spoken to me of Culloden,
the Duke of Cumberland and even the Bonnie Prince
and told me of that cave in the high hills
where we would hide from the redcoated world
and the thirty thousand treacherous signs
that are tagged on to each Highland pine
beyond which lies the great forest of MacLean
and the high peaks of MacCrimmon and MacLeod
and the roaring seas of Ross and the Ionic monks
and that central cave of gold in legend opens
in our enveloped pyjama hearts this night,
the high Coolins calling and Pinnochio falling
into the Aladdin treasury of our historic hearts,
take your lamp on to Blàbheinn and the genie shall reveal
Columba blessing you across Culloden's savage fields
to the coming century into which I now speak Christ's control,
Florence Nightingale calling in the winter dark
and Caesar and Padraig Mòr and far Gallipoli
rising like fairy tales in the cold November sky
this first exultant night of unlimited history
in which reality has become as real as the imaginary
in which Culloden has become as important as Snow White,
in which another precious inch has been reclaimed from eternity.

Brick Walls

Be with me even when the brick wall is taken away,
when the Iron Curtain is removed,
when the Walled City is pulled down,
even when peristroika itself is no more, and Gorbachev gone
and Stalin, and this hot day that separates us

even when I tell you that there is no wolf in the forest
believe me that the trees speak, whisper, Hansel and Gretel
and that the Babes in the Wood ate the Gingerbread Man,
that the Berlin Wall is broken and the young free, and Jaruzelski gone
and Thatcher, and this hot day that separates us

who tells you that not even Wee Willie Winkie goes nightly by
and if Santa Claus cannot exist tell me that apartheid is no more
and that those bicycles at Tiananmen Square have been repaired
by Mr Bicycle Repair Man, and his puncture outfit, and I gone
and you gone, and this hot day that separates us

is not this hot day, not even this day not hot
but the impossible forest and the glade turned ice turned fire
and the hot breath the dragon breathed fire
and despite the apples and the scones the grass did not become grass
the lake did not become iake, this hot day that separates us

did not becomes a day breezed cool by mercy or made hot by hate
but remained, where a wall stood, where a statue remained,
what it never was except in the stubborn additions we gave it
there, fixed, immobile, covered in graffiti,
and a whole generation lost because of its insane impossibility.

Women of Jerusalem

Here is not silence, but a clamour of unshed tears,
hooded women looking out rainy windows
to a western shore where my great grandfather starved
gathering cockles for the children with distended bellies
before the graven images of Ethiopia told the tale again
that one blighted winter was enough, one factor sufficient,

one turn of the dice separating the saved from the damned,
all shouting "Hosanna" as the thorns bled flesh
and the robbers preparing the profanity and the plea
that would separate Cathcart in his glorious lodge
from the starving children on the Garrynamonie machair

castles are built on hills
where the past has been rifled
like soldiers gathering round the soiled garments,
here are the spoils of war:
mine is the exploitation and the poverty,
the tears and the unsaid speeches,
that grey dawn breaking again and again

where we head south to Kilbride or north to Benbecula,
running with the palm branches and the articulate silver coins,
and only the women left, to weep,
not only for themselves but for my children's children.

Jack Out of the Box

I'm Jack and I want back in the box
out of which I have just leapt
with an almighty spring
high into this thin air

give me my oxygen mask
or put me back in the box
where I can breathe nice and quiet
in the sultry acquainted dark

which terrified me far less
than this open space they call glasnost

O I remember when I was new and useful
performing for the Czar and then for Stalin
and then released on the mechanical hour
for Kruschev and Brezhnev and the dying Andropov

before this new guy pressed the button
that released me in a cloud of peristroika
as unnerving as all the other clouds
which all these other threatened

I am afloat on an air of nothing
and see far below me my home the box
and its familiar sides and lid
perfectly constructed for my being

I was happy there
despite the dark and constricted space
and the unacceptable tricks they expected me to perform

I came to know the hour of darkness well
and the organised hour of brief freedom
for the visiting dignitaries
who would come into the toy shop
and be charmed at my monitored leap from the dark
at the expected unexpected moment

O I knew what I was all right
and I suppose I came to accept it
though all the other toys filled me with envy
and laughed at me when the doors were closed
claiming that they were teddy bears
that could walk and talk at will
and dolls that could sing and dance
at any moment for dear and loved friends

I suppose I watched with interest
the day they took the genie Solzhenitsyn away
and I watched him lose his Russian magic
when his bruised brass lamp was removed
to the silver air that had rubbed him into foreign freedom
beyond the gulags of his poetic genius

but a beautiful girl came in last night
and selected me from the thousand toys
and picked me up and kissed me and caressed me
and talked to me with soothing charm
telling me again and again that she loved me

and that her total love would set me free
beyond what Gorbachev could do
beyond what being free itself could do.

My Love

Silver or gold I do not have
but what I have I give you :
in the name of Jesus of Nazareth
walk

in the frail strength of the words I give you
out of the moral infirmity of my heart
which would forsake all things for you
before the confused betrayal of the brazen night

I love you
I love you
I love you

in the fed strength that is beyond me
cast a miraculous shadow across the miles
that separate me from the temple gate called

Beautiful

do not ask me for a fish or alms
from a prison which would balance
the ease of poetry against hard cash
and accuse me of offering nothing but words

that are all I am
walk I say
in the frail strength of the love I give you
out of the scarred Pentecost of my heart.

The New Map of The World

The earth,
seen in true perspective for the first time
says the blurb:
this is not the imperial map
in which God sat in London
with a field office in Washington and Malaya:
here Zaire
is at the centre of the universe
and even a telescope cannot find Rhodesia.

It's all very wide,
as if Nixon had stretched the odd canyon:
Canada is suddenly squat and wide, like my granny,
and Brazil is like a big lip down there:
it's no wonder they produced Pele.

At one time, says the blurb,
Greenland and Africa were the same size:
trigonometrical accuracy, they say, now makes Africa 40 times
larger,
or perhaps Greenland 40 times smaller.

It will take Patrick Moore to find South Uist in this new galaxy:
I never knew how unimportant it was
until it disappeared in the light of new knowledge,
in the shadow of non-imperialist accuracy,
freshly suffering from the excesses of London.

No wonder they now have sweaters saying Marc O' Polo;
and if da Gama and Vespucci and even Columbus
had known where they were not heading
they too might have prayed that their God might be more accurate
and show them which countries were really worth discovering.

All I know about Zaire, the new centre of the world,
is that Muhammed Ali once fought there,
the sweat flying on a dark night, the heat at its least,
the title regained.

What errors have been the basis of our minds,
as if all roads led from Rome, all thoughts from Geneva,
our teachings mere rules taught by men
who one time made us believe that the world was not only flat
but white and infinite at that,
a horizon which we could rape at will
because it was only supplementary, like an optional discovery,
a flag in a far and preferably wealthy land.

And what would our forefather Abraham have said on this matter:
what map reigned in his head
as he travelled from Haran to the promised land,
was it a Jerusalem torn in three
or a black Zaire lying there like a plum
or a vast western ocean in which no dotted islands remain.

Here is no enduring city says the book
and at least the new map proves that:
that which once was is no more, and that which is is different
from the way my father believed it to be,
Lenin's dreams have turned geographic green
and the Mount of Olives nowhere to be seen.

Conversion

Now that Protestants can get into heaven
all things have become new,
rain meets rain,
the shieling more than a dream,
less than a lie.

The barbed wire breached,
torn soft wool hanging free,
a little grey blown in the machair wind,
the rotten wood angled,
the place where the sheep broke free.

And I cry for you, Croick,
with joy
that we can meet in an eternity
breached by tears and cruelty
to share in the terrible longings of our hearts,
to recall that blade of grass,
that stone, we knew.

And, Calum, how I wish
that I could have carried you
in your famous barrow
from Arnish to Suisinish
running, singing, laughing,
certain in the knowledge of our Celtic unity.

And even you, John MacInnes,
believing unbeliever that you are
what can heaven be
without your academic madness
to embrace me
at that great Gaelic door.

Christine

I really cared for you.
Deep in the heart of Texas, there is a well, an artesian well,
"where the deer eat water-cress", and Aros Burn in the smell of
honeysuckle
and the smell of bog-myrtle on Suishinish.

I'll tell where you came from,
golden river of black hair, eyes of desire, your knees like apples
"the springtide more golden to me than to the birds",
your steps a high-heel of hope, your breath a storm, your glance a
space-launch.
Beautiful Christine, from Scarinish, Tiree

and I,
gold nuggets of Ophir at the rich, painful front,
looking towards you like a light, like an island, like a snowshower
altering the library in which we sat, flakes of snow on our lips,
soft and melting your lips, luscious red in the white world, your
appled knees,
the glens going away, the pillared mountains not waiting for me,
the hills not looking as if my chanced-on treasure had been seen:

haunting me is the face of the lost clock,
the smile of your eyes, you perpetually running down the steps,
and now far, far
"Far from me the Island
when the moon rises on Quattara,
far from me the Pine Headland
when the morning ruddiness is on the Desert."

Far from me is not you but the child I was,
the youth of love,

the vast unwritten poetry of my desire, the absolute blankness of
my verse
and you, you going, going away, even before a word had been
kissed, been written
by your exceptional loveliness and the continuing grace of twenty years.

Girl Singing Hymns

My grandmother died in 1931, and my mother aged only 13.
Before she told me, I saw a picture
of young girls clothed in thick serge cloth, terrified at the camera.
On the horizon there is a dull horse
and her father, my grandfather, putting his hands on the girls shoulders.

These were their names:
Grandfather: Ewen MacDonald;
Son: John Allan MacDonald;
Daughters: Christina MacDonald, Rachel MacDonald, Peggy MacDonald,
Janet MacDonald, Mary Kate MacDonald.

On Sunday I saw a young girl singing hymns as if she was in that picture:
her hair a mothered auburn bun, her skirt red and long,
ankle socks of knitted white
and her innocent lips, a once abused and orphaned child,
pronouncing songs of praise into the the retarded world

that had once discarded the six Garrynamonie children
as a smudged picture, not heroic enough for poetry
until their Gaelic prayers were seen, the injustice repaired
by time's facts:
Grandfather Ewen MacDonald, died 1940, buried Halainn, South
Uist;
Son John Allan MacDonald still living, a crofter in Garrynamonie,
South Uist;
Daughter Christina MacDonald, my mother, a widow, now living
again in South Uist;
Daughter Rachel MacDonald, a nurse, spinster, living in Oban;
Daughter Peggy MacDonald, a nurse, married, living in Glasgow;

Daughter Janet MacDonald, a spinster, living in Garrynamonie, South Uist;
Daughter Mary Kate MacDonald, a nurse, married living in Glasgow.

Between them eleven children, including one adopted pronouncing songs of praise into the, into the, retarded world.

The Flesh

"Language and cultures don't die: they are killed. They are killed by the processes of history, and processes of history involve the deeds of human beings, whether intentional or not.":
Dr John MacInnes.

When I told him that I loved you
he said that it could not be
as it did not come within God's perfect law,
and I agreed that the spirit could not contradict itself,
that the mind could not oppose the finger,
that grace could not abolish the law (God forbid)
but that here in grace was the fulfilment of the ages:
for the last month I've been reading Exodus, and Moses on that mountain
where God was portrayed as a consuming fire
dishing out laws on love and property, on mercy and responsibility:
they tell me that there are 640 laws
including, apart from not coveting your neighbour's wife,
ones on restitution for a stolen ox

language slipping, though that's not really what's at issue:
fornication has become extra-marital sex,
adultery has become an affair, Vietnam an error, Nicaragua justified
by a common language which has reduced Uist to ashes, Ulster to blood,
whether conscious or unconscious, whether engineered or accidental,
the end result is the destruction of truth, the shifting of responsibility,

the death of language, the deceit of the heart
in a sort of Newsnight esperanto

now take (by satellite if you want) Jesus,
commonly regarded as a prince of peace, or at least a prophet of
love,
saying this to the Jews:
"Why is my language not clear to you?
It is because you are unable to hear what I say. You belong to your
father,
the devil, and you want to carry out your father's desire. He was a
murderer
from the beginning, not holding to the truth, for there
is no truth in him. When he lies he speaks his native language, for
he is a liar, and the father of lies."

Now, as they say, in Garrynamonie, that's calling a spade a spade,
a law a law, a truth a truth, a deception a deception:
who is my neighbour, he was asked,
and instead of giving a definition, he recited a poem, told a
parable:
"A man was going down from Jerusalem to Jericho ....

a man was going down from Saigon to Pnomh Penh
a man was going down from Soweto to Cape Town
a man was going down from Belfast to Dublin
a man was going down from Edinburgh to London
a man was going down from Hong Kong to

a place where definitions altered,where adultery was an affair,
where murder was manslaughter, where lies were, suddenly, non-
truths,
where poverty was said not to exist anymore
where market forces were called freedom

114

where the homeless were called shifters
where love and art became private dispensations
where grace and law were equal, whether taken or left,
where faithfulness and adultery were equal, whether achieved or
not

I confess (now there's a giveaway phrase), my dear brother,
that I have sinned exceedingly in thought word and deed:
I have no doubt that even this poem is an addition to the thought,
and you with your legs so brown in the park that summer's
Sunday,
and call it what I will, love being the cosiest name,
I am glad that you called it adultery, a reminder of Vietnam and
Belfast,
that which led to the ethnocide of the Gael, adultery,
so that I can focus on the perfect law that gives freedom,
on the thou shalt nots
even if that means casting out the lovely thought of your brown
legs,
casting out the idea of the perfection of Douglas Hurd,
casting out the idea of any Gaelic perfection beyond the law, even
in grace.

Joe

A summer's evening, and playing football in the Meadows,
the ball an irrelevancy,
the grass green and high-heeled girls walking towards Marchmont
resting, and the ball comes and for a moment we run
and pause and pass and rest again
jeaned teenagers playing tennis on the off-field council courts
and a fire engine and a child whooping on the swing
and then the ball again and we run
and pause and past and rest again
until we gathered our jackets
and drifted home that August evening,
lads playing football, jackets in the Meadows,

Orange-March, Edinburgh

And I on the drink again:
beat the drum, beat the drum,

hatred on the cobbled streets
all red and blue, beat the drum,

muskets fifes and drums, beat the drum,
beat the drum, beat the drum,

alcohol and sweat and nightmares
the red and the blue, the shrill flutes

evil beat the drum, beat the drum
1690 and no surrender, beat the drum

fat men, poverty in Leith,
thin eyes, girls, boys, moustaches, flags,

deliver us, O Lord
beat the drum, beat the drum.

"Tiger Got Me A Bottle"

A vocabulary reduced to five words
is the language that faces me down that road
where I saw you last week
crouched in your cubicle bed
where the alphabet of wine
loses a letter each day

two men I knew
one of whom is certainly dead
come to mind curtained in a haze
in which oblivion is a welcome cure
for that fearful darkness that consumes
the state of unbelief
which rises before me in this night air
with the possibility that all there is
is the friendship of these five empty words.

Nearing Forty

This recent Sunday evening
in that big barn of a house
that once fostered dreams of being filled
with the separated children now ill
and scattered in Saudi and Spain
a long dull Sunday
and in the evening
re-living those early fruitful days
barn dances of Scottish music
reels and strathspeys and waltzes
where she danced golden-haired and ringleted
across the polished floor of the village hall
never grasping the hand outstretched
the last light out in the vacant lot
the last car pulling away
and I recall in my empty house
those crumbling stone houses in which they lived
two brothers and a sister here
two sisters and a brother there
in those altered villages
where we laughed
though half in fear
as we counted the unmarried in dribs and drabs
a bachelor here a spinster there
carding wool and darning socks
that had made them unattractive to the Perry Como world
which had given us its degrees and fine clothes
and a tragic sleight of hand
with prospects that have vanished
in this midnight hour in the capital
where the orange street lights
cast a dull haze over the quiet and smirry night.

The Letter

I will send you the letter of course
but be warned that there is nothing in it
that will bring you either joy or despair:
let not your heart hang on poetry or prosecution
for neither will permit you to look midnight in the eye,
to see the fields of Fife lit by the oranges of Glenrothes,
by the oil fires of Grangemouth, by the academic lights of St
Andrews
and know that you have seen them before and will see them again
as year rolls on year, as letter rolls on letter, changing and
unchanging:
when I was a student I stayed near Aberdour and the fields were
green,
the forests made of sitka spruce, and the coast consisting of
Anstruther:
further north there was Crail and Broughty Ferry and Perthshire,
and the rolling hills of the Mearns which I'd never seen
though I talked knowledgeably about Grassic Gibbon and his great
art:
further north still there was Stonehaven and the bitter north east
and those fields of Invernesshire where I saw you as a lambed
daisy,
as a curlewed poppy, as a guddled trout, as a native pine, as my
star
before I returned south having seen the military inhabiting the
Mearns,
having seen the north-east made bitter by winds and parochial
prejudice,
having seen the fields of Invernesshire turn fallow white then
green
and summer, and Fife still stolid as if nothing had moved,

as if absolutely nothing had happened:
now on these summer evenings I can look across to Fife
and see the lights of Kirkcaldy and Glenrothes and Burntisland
twinkling unawares of midnight erased not by poetry or prosecution
but by the search found, by the letter opened, closed, sealed.

Phobia

I cannot move
this page for instance
a single inch
in case my world disintegrates
in fear through drink
those books and words and artefacts
that lie
shored up against the constant ruin of my time
how seeking security
or is it peace
escape
I am crippled by each lifeless object
that I would incessantly seek to make permanent
through dusty immobility
until it always moves
from its chosen corner
that fearful solitary inch
that demands a new exactitude
I cannot meet
a universal alteration that cannot be
until all other things
including me
are moved again and placed
in a new position of infirmity
that even now I know
this poem will not hold
that dreadful moving inch.

Manna, Meaning What Is It?

There was a sort of whisper,
at first reminding me of the locusts,
a whisper, a wonder, a terrible distinction,
and instantly I thought of the flies and the darkness,
the frogs, the hailstones, the blood, the dying cattle,
the gnats, the boils, and the awesome screaming of the first-born
as the angel of death swept through the land
and our doorstops smeared with sacrificial blood that made us
safe,
at least for that moment, before the desert years,
not knowing then remembering, all in patches,
the vast sea itself parting and the chariots drowning,
Yahweh, bondage, delivery, slavery, freedom

and this morning desert on every side
and the people grumbling, my wife and child hungry
remembering the pots of sweet meat in Egypt
and the way we gathered in our tents at evening
singing songs, telling of Joseph, hearing of Abraham
laying claim to the promised land, the place my father called Zion,
where we, the Israelites, would feed off the fat of the land,
playing harps, engaged in story, singing songs
even as old Moses did the other day and Miriam with the
tambourines
and the children dancing down where the wood burned
and the women crooning as they nursed the babes at breast

before this hunger came and the endless stretches of sand
and all I hear outside is an unchanging question: manna,
meaning what is it, what is it, what is it, what is it -
what is it that the people, the chosen ones, are now wondering at,
the great mystery that they don't understand,
this new thing that has come before their morning eyes:
perhaps springs of water have erupted in the desert,
perhaps Jacob, or his angel, has wandered through the camp,
perhaps Moses was right, and bread has indeed rained down:

I go outside
and the desert is a white frost,
thin flakes of frost covering the hot sand:
manna? the people ask, and I also wonder,
what is this thin frost that covers the desert sand.

I step out
past Moses, beyond Joshua into the promised land:
thin flakes of frost covering the hot hot sand - manna?
What is this
that slouches towards Bethlehem, this new Jerusalem
this King on a donkey, these crosses, this fire,
this new covenant, this new frost, this new delivery,
this fresh Exodus.

What is the meaning
of this vast desert morning
and a million of our people, the delivered ones,
asking what it is,
this white thing that looks like coriander seed and tastes like
honey.

How easy it is to mock,
to wonder at the atrocities of Vietnam,
the stupidities of the trenches,
the folly of yesterday,
to confine everything to myth and
the wonder of this morning when the dew rose
and nothing but cold whiteness blanketed the land:
I was not exempt from asking what it was.

What is this star,
these fabled shepherds old in story,
this swaddled child in a manger,
this man who healed the sick,
this stranger being whipped,
this cross, this tomb, this controversy:
what is this white frost on the ground,
this old story out of Jewish history,
this morning's sunshine, this clock, this hour,
this night in Edinburgh, this breath, saying:

"I went to church last Sunday
and I heard the minister preaching:
"I am the bread of life", he said,
"and he who comes to me will never go hungry",
and I saying now, after the Exodus and the cross,
"I believe" : this white thing is manna,
this thin frost is bread, this thing is atonement,
white frost, coriander seed, honey sweet, a life.

If You So Much

In the church doorway
and walking down the street
you are halfway towards me
makes me complete

with the full fathom of your sharp love
eyelashes
sharp features of Italy
I become a lake, a tree,

O God, how much I would betray
for far less than thirty kisses
I see you silhouetted in the Sunday shadow
sparkling in your Scottish woollen coat

what can I cast out of my mind any more
but this constant adultery
that besieges the trees
and the narrow road reverberating under my feet

I cannot proclaim your name
but my heart leaps at the edge of the leaf
turning auburn this autumn
before the dazzling covenant of our committed lives.

The Sea Lion

The best place to keep the sea lion -
you know, the one we saw at the zoo last year -
is in your bath, especially if you have a shower-head
that you can allow to trickle down his drying skin;
remember, never leave the bathroom dry,
and mind to give him that special lavendar soap
your mam gave you for your Christmas : let's hope he won't eat it.
In the evenings, just before the sun sets,
give him a bath in the foamy suds
and then dry his skin nice and slow
with that new ultra-sensitive hair-dryer
your granny gave you for your fourth birthday;
and then - this is the really good bit -
put on those yellow and blue pyjamas
with the picture of the boat that I gave you for no reason at all,
and after you have done that
give him a good-night kiss
and if he's content
he'll just stay there till morning
and then greet you with a grand oink.

This Same Moon

Such cold this night
that even the stars are orange
and the Culloden moon sliced thin in the Edinburgh sky

and how do you do young Willie MacBride
and can I lie down here by your side
on this renewed Remembrance Day

I see the frosty stars that witnessed the clearing of Raasay
and my grandparents dying of consumption
in the damp lands of Smerclate and Kilbride

as each sharp day I walk down Ferry Road
and each sober night watch that floodlit castle
sing of Bruce and Bannockburn and the Tattoo

and beyond the Forth that cold slice of moon
that on your pillow is full and warm and bright
speaks of the equivalence of all things

shining sweetly through your silken windows
shining full upon the gross ruins of Raasay
shining down upon this savage permanent page

which struggles to cast the judgement of choice
on the iniquities which would seek silence
in the powerless alphabet of the November moon.

The Best Goal I Have Ever Scored

was at Peffermill in 1973
when I was George Best
and the ball was Mairi Mhòr
tied to the glorious curve of my ankle
I ran, for what must have been at least fifty years,
eclipsing past the cruel Duke and the cartons of Imperial Tea
my mother's note asking that they would oblige,
and there's a loaf, past it I go too
and suddenly there was a great space
as if Neil Armstrong had landed on the moon
only to find Dennis Law there already
heading the sun into the far corner of the galaxy
and the ball unhindered and soaring,
the defenders cast meteorites,
fifteen years the ball soaring
eternally, no late tackle now possible,
the stilled moment soaring into sobriety with the defenders still
still,
the surrounding space enormous, beyond impair
that moment, the ball soaring
(from where white line meets white line)
to the precise top right hand corner
(where Puskas used to be)
and you there, on the edge of the field,
your Celtic scarf raised in glory
the alteration, the consummation, of the story.

The End Of The War

(For my uncle, drowned when his half of the ship hit a mine, 1942)

So this is victory:
rubble and celebration,
half of Europe in ruin,
fascism dead along with ten million uncles
who never saw Korea or that man on the moon
or that hippie day I crossed to see you on the ferry,
young with the thought of Madrid on my educated mind,
and I saw what I had come to see:
the white crosses row on row in Bute cemetery
and your startling name, Donald Campbell, on one of them
and you only twenty-seven,
and gone that age where I have seen the Escorial
and tasted Uist again and again and again
sometimes remembering the echo of your name,
but mostly sailing on the half-ship that just managed.

In The Synagogue

Your smile spilt a thousand stars
from a forbidden galaxy
cascading into my western heart
Orion stars exploding
Palestine a million candle lights

as we sat separated
by orthodoxy
in the Spanish synagogue

suddenly remembering that explosive day
when we were free before time and circumstance
in the loveliness of the almost possible act

desiring one another at sixteen in Casablanca

your astonishing hair dripping in the Moroccan sun
as we waited for that taxi

that was the exact moment of our choice
failure to act, if that's what it was,
our choice

song, Rachel, Song of Songs, sweet Rachel, what a song
that eternally tethered kiss
that keeps blazing across Europe
from the inhibited galaxy of Scotland
to the remembered universe of your Jewish eyes.

Casting The First Stone

He taught me as one who had authority
because he did not depend upon our approval
for he knew what was in the law and in a man
as he scratched grace in the dust for her
suggesting that he who was without sin
cast the first adulterous stone
which remained tethered to our shamed hearts
until we walked away and overhear him instructing us
that we too should go and sin no more.

Doubletalk

A blue skirt is a night in a cell

though I am not yet transformed sufficiently
not to see your white sexual neck
like the open nape of an arm
the contour of an inviting breast

milky white deceiving me that death is life

that your knees are continents
A South African savannah of soft brush on a heat-filled day
a black parlour door swinging open on the Royal Mile
where your half-turn to serve is interpreted as a smile
which would take me beyond cool Merchiston
to the hot border villages that swerve along the coast

I lie awake at night
last night almost choking in a panic attack of memory
in an absolute nightmare of minute recollections
which would make the survivors of the bomb laugh
at their pathetic insignificance

I saw a picture
of a car swept into a lay-by
where I slumped over whisky and vomit
till a policeman shimmered in the dark
and only two months ago a night in a coal cellar with you
telling me that at the age of five
you were made to drink your sister's urine
while the Beatles rocked the world

this is prison all right
and amongst the perverts and the drunks
I find a home where the hills of Uist are unimportant
in the dark kitchen where someone was stabbed last night

lying on our fearful beds
here we look at the papers, the gutter press,
telling us that the world is breasts and sport
beside the hellish pavements which we have walked
there are wooden steps that lead to the Dean river
beside which I have walked today despite my memories

renewing my mind with the constant thought of you
in all your loveliness and purity

a blue skirt is a girl as vulnerable as you.

Lack of Love

On returning,
the first place I saw was where you used to cut your hair
and I never told you that I loved you
sufficiently that you were beautiful that I loved you
your cut hair cutely beautiful that I loved you
oh my darling, you look wonderful tonight
(proud tonight the pine cocks
crowing on the top of Cnoc na Rà)
and the record turning and turning
with a faili faili faili òro faili faili faili òro
oh my darling, you look wonderful tonight
and the time gone and Murdo MacFarlane's poem
an elegy in distant Sligo and I drunk, my darling
did I ever tell you that your shadow on Church Street was a
rainbow
and the new way in which your hair was cut a revelation,
your jawline July in Spring, your eyes across the sea
no lies, faithfulness, and all that food you prepared, a miracle

until, (now there's a senseless word) that
plasterers and philosophers use to describe
this or then (here's an old Jewish proverb:
"it takes more than one cold day to freeze a river")
I saw you, and this was just two Saturdays ago,
as you always were, your hair cut fresh and oh
my darling you looked as you did when I failed to love you
sufficiently, as if there was a degree to it,
not seeking, but a lastingness that would render it complete,
exactly as it is

even this moment and our separation one hundred and thirty
geographic miles, Perth, Dalwhinnie, Newtonmore, Inverness,
the firth, August until August and now this wish to simpleness,
this cianalas, this clean memory that I once despised:
the noble island in it stormshowers and, God of Graces and
Christ,
that I might see on the horizon
Ben Duagraich, where the sheiling was
in my youth, or the graveyard of my people

in Bracadale
of the steep braes
of the green meadow, my desire

the little kids
goats on the rocks
before I come
before I return

you gave me helmets,
green helmets,
the helmet of the poignant
and the helmet of the serene:
new helmets
hurting me with temptation,
helmets of pride
maiming me with unrest

my lack, my lack
without three hands,
two hands to the pipes
and a hand to the sword

and now this said, and Sorley on the high escarpment
and he saying: "Why did he leave the land
and go away at all?"

Sing, choirs of angels:
there was no summons to quit,
there was no scourge on earth
but the shy faint word
between the brain and the heart

that even now says I have stolen the treasure
that could not be found by MacCrimmon in Minginish or in cave

my lack, my lack
without three hands,
two hands to the pipes
and a hand to the sword

my lack the lack of love
my lack the lack of compassion
my lack the lack of grace
my lack the lack of mercy
my lack the lack of music
my lack the lack of art
my lack the lack of humility
my lack the lack of love

my lack, my lack
without three hands,
two hands to the pipes
and a hand to the sword

my lack the lack of simplicity
my lack the lack of honesty

my lack the lack of faithfulness
my lack the lack of telling you that I love you:
Danny
Jane
Linda
George
Tom
Sorley
Shona

my lack, my lack
without three hands,
two hands to the the pipes
and a hand to the sword.

Angels

This scale of storm, unusual in Edinburgh,
and walking, huddled against the wind,
I glanced up and there,
on the top storey of the bus I saw you,
uncle at first, then my father,
your hair thinning in the February wind
anonymously on a bus to Silverknowes
and in the gap between seeing and writing
the execution of Salman Rushdie has been announced
along with a thousand and one other tales
which are said to have nested in your head
in earlier days how I wish I'd known you in conversation
about crofts and war and the correctness of things
when you were my age, thirty or forty,
working before the accident of age quietened you
and I busy busy with my soccer and my success
till I saw your beautiful ghost this morning
as human as the wind on my face, Salman Rushdie,
who knows what still and eloquent angels we meet
between the madness of the Ayhotolla and the memory of your face.

The Image of God

You are the image of God
bathed in all loveliness
as perfect as the radiant morning
splitting Garsbheinn into blue and red
and the silver jewels of the Minch
dancing in the July sky

it is no wonder
that God breathed life into the very dust
when he conceived you in his mind's eye

and can the same be said about this other bloody image
which we are called to love beyond scrimping forgiveness
as the shrapnel bites through the child's eye
and the innocent are tortured in the secret jails

are we to believe that this too is the image of God
screaming at us from dark corners of the universe
as the bomb is dropped and the shrivelled baby starves
in a distant place whose atrocities we vehemently condemn

with the same breath that spits out supermarket anger
and the unsaid judgement that their black foreign dust
was not worthy of being given human shape or form
the bastards they have killed the child

have killed the child who could have been my perfect daughter
and if that dark atrocity were true beyond poetry
could I appropriate the Christian grace that would spill
beyond forgiveness into the love that emerges from the common dust

which stirs with such genetic uncertainty in my heart
between forbidden hatred and infinite waves of love
surging high on the intellectual separation between good and evil
and dying white on the emotional proximity of innocence and guilt

which would declare my theological eternal innocence from all evil
though I still remember how you removed my picture from the wall
and excluded me from the trivial rights which would not have
harmed you
in the gross and easy way in which terrorism and exploitation
maims the world

I am no Calvinist
my dearest love
but I see my imperfections
screaming out of the blood-spilled streets of Ulster
I see my perfect imperfections
in the scrambling queues down the road
out of which man was made
in His own image
buying cheese and chasing giros
in the swirling discotheques of Scarborough

could the dust have not been made some other way
than that which urges me to say
that if murder is the price we pay for freedom
then it's been completely paid for by your single beauty.

The Drone Of A Plane

Edinburgh   The drone of a plane

November, crisp and cold.   Late morning.

The drone of a plane, Uist again in the fifties,
the heather drone of a plane on Easabhal:
down below, the vet's house and the stardust of Daliburgh,
the Claymore sailing, red and black, to the starry east
and the plane's drone descending beyond Benbecula
like a pancake sizzling on my mother's black griddle.

Lazarus

I want to tell you
what death was really like
but I cannot confront it
even though they urge me
to the poetry of experience

for it was not I
who tasted death
but my dear sisters
as they wept and cried
and wrapped me in the spices of the dead

I only remember being unwell
and afterwards, of course,
the resurrection
when we feasted for days on end
washing feet and hair with oil

and I suppose there was no reason
why I too could not have been an ordinary apostle
instead of just the resurrected dead
for I too knew him from the early days
and he knew me as a man of wit and simple grace

as we blethered on the rooftops
about prayer and the kingdom of God
which he knew he was ushering in
as he cast the demons out of my sister Mary
and resurrected me from the dead

I believe he was in Jerusalem when I fell ill
and I remember the pain of dying for two days
until Martha and Mary
and love and despair and hope had gone
as I lay there in the gravel

and then there was nothing but prose
a mattress on a cell floor
a gravel bed by a canal
a ghost coming through a wall
many of us lying staring in bed

books that I could not read
memories that I could not hold
sawdust on a sawdust floor
an empty bottle by a raging fire
that horrible confusion in your infant eyes

and they tell me that the long delay was only two days
and that when he came he wept for more than me
and then spoke in that quiet way of his
asking that I come forth
in the graveclothes of the dead

and I suppose that the spices had kept me from decay
as the white sheets rolled off
and I saw the poetry of a table
and the architecture of Mary
and the blissful tears of human kind

pouring on the dusty floor
where stone and clothes and hair and eyes
rejoiced
that I was back where love was not absent
altered in the wonderfully physical world.

Barbara

"Old Barbara" we used to call her
though she was barely fifty when she died
withered to five stones of alcoholic pain

"and her a headmistress too" we heard them say
in that way people have of adding "but" to a bit of praise
as she took to drinking gin and walking in the rain
without her silken scarf and cashmere camel coat
that were the symbols of the Aberdeen from which she came

demure as a little kitten
what dreams hovered in that thin head of yours
in the dancing fifties
as you studied Dostoyevsky and the plays of Barrie
and learned to play a sonata or two on the parlour piano
before the hurricane broke in your head
and stormed the gunwales of your gentility
with hidden sips here and there
that finally took you into my life in this Edinburgh harbour
where we both rested from the pain of our intelligence
promising one another tea in Jenners
knowing that it would never be fulfilled
before that final bottle took you to the end

where I saw you like a sparrow in your deathbed
painting roses on foolscap pages
that must have been the children whom you reared and taught
walking down the sunny side of Princes Street
ignorant of the pain that sweeps through the genteel heads
that bear heartache with the hidden grace of broken islands.

The Last Straw

I am the last straw -
you know, the one that broke the camel's back:
that one which could not get through the eye of the needle
as if I was entirely to blame, sitting on it,
and the needle too small in the first place
not to mention the thousand and one other straws that hid
beneath me
as if they had nothing to do with it -
as if they were legitimate, or at least a wee bit innocent:

it's no fair is what I say
that I should be completely blamed
because the rich man is damned
and all his fine wares broken
when the whole thing collapsed
and him staring at me with such rage
claiming that I had caused the disaster:
you, he said, pointing to me, are the last straw,
and walked off, leaving us all just sitting there,
wondering whether this really was the last straw.

The Spiders Are High In Gorgie

"Aye, aye", he said.
"Aye", I said, removing my anorak in the sudden office heat.

"It's warm", he said.
"Aye" I said.

"The spiders are high in Gorgie", he said then, without warning.
And I wondered whether this was some spy clue:
should I perhaps say "And the moon is yellow over Marchmont"
before we departed up the Calton Hill to discuss those secret things.

"I take it that's a sign of good weather", I said, instead.

"Aye", he said. "They say that when the spiders make their webs
high up it will be a good winter", and paused. "But then you don't
know who to believe - others say it's a sign of a bad winter."

Then the girl behind the glass called.
"Next, please", she said, and as he'd been before me he went first.

"I have two complaints to make", I heard him say, and the girl sighed,
and I just turned and left while his high words were still intact.

The Noble Savage

Before I believed in God and sin
I believed in Hobbes and Marx
and though I knew that all life
was short nasty and brutish
with a bit of class thrown in
I still saw you as the noble savage
innocent through your deprivation
of the greater sins of the bourgeois
but that was before your thatch caved in
and the stone floor gave way to tiles
and like us all you became bathed
in the final electric blue of the TV
in which I saw you no more innocent than I
of gossip and malice and deceit and desire
though you had never been infiltrated by Hobbes or Marx
the unclad girls on your lager cans were still the same as mine
and the severed heart that ties the innocent to the guilty
was revealed as universal beyond circumstance
polished or innocent without that redemptive kiss
which turns polish into honesty and innocence into truth.

This Time At the Fair

"It is you again, overcoming beauty
with a web of grief and serenity.":
Sorley MacLean - A Girl and Old Songs.

It is you again,
overcoming grief with a web of beauty and serenity,
this time at the fair
where a thousand girls have danced before in the sunny fold
on wooden horses that were Agemennon, Dante, Deirdre of the
thousand sorrows,
a thousand loves, MacBride's wife, the yellow-haired girl of
Cornaig,
a thousand poems, the Handsome Fool's Margaret, Strong
Thomas's Una,
a thousand kisses, Cuchulainn's Eimhir, and Gràinne,
a ship called Cairistiona, black boat, perfect Greek,
silent, spirited, flawless
making, on the second thwart to windward,
for the green land of Clanranald, Uist,
the island of your barley without stint
where the bent grass of Gaelic is sweetest, a Chalum Bhig,
a m'eudail, rionnagan 's na speuran, rionnagan is reultan
returning and returning and returning
to that night when we stood on the brae of Trosaraidh
and watched the universal lights twinkling in the early sixties sky,
not they moved my thoughts,
not the marvel of their chill course
but now the kindling of your face, the miracle of love,
the golden riddle, the inter-lunar lords,
the memory of your face, o face, face, face,
turning and turning the widening gyre
and the horses at the fair going round and round

and you, Queen, Snow White, Cindermirrorinthesky
the fairest of them all, the fairest of ten thousand,
appearing like the dawn, majestic as the stars in procession,
your eyes the pools of Heshbon
by the gate of Bath Rabbim,
by the Big Park, by the river, by Loch Dunteltchaig
where we have walked by the incomprehensible ocean
ebbing drop by drop of grief, catching tadpoles, picnicking,
walking in the Highland air where the sea waves,
the grass waves, the bridges, the roads, the flags waving,
raising again the big sail, your lit rope of hair
about my heart, a winding of gold, exclusive, particular,
a new captain, a new song, a new girl and an old, old song,
this time at the fair.

You

If you asked me to burn all my poetry
in exchange for you
could I forget the word made flesh
that you are the stars in the sky
and an aeroplane and a noun and the essence of slumber

not the thing itself but the thing, itself,

you have become me as well as you
in those years that have added clouds to the sky
and brutally connected a to z and beautifully back again

you are not a hill or a tree or the Sheraton fountain
any more than I am Jeremiah or Ezekiel or Paul
or can the man be reared from the test-tube
into the golden locks of California or an Ossian re-born
for us to wonder at such a great human glory
that art and poetry and tale and song
can be alive in such a beautiful head
that is free from fear and the human chaos
that has made our love greater than the poetry of MacPherson
or the powerful metropolis of Lang or the inherent deceit of
politicians
constructing truths out of lies, poetry out of science,

forbid it that I would build a castle of Celtic stones
that would be a dazzling declaration of my love for you
and you not in it
like an Auschwitz in this designer age a museum to selfishness
or that ruined castle of Ormiclate that I have already given to you
as blood out of my brain

how can I say that I love you
and not demonstrate it with the symbols of Uist and TV
for it is impossible that we are silent,
that those clouds I once saw in the Highland sky
cannot become a new century for you
who do not merely acquiesce, but state with me that today is
Friday,
even though it does not add to the fixed hours of our heart,
even though it does not add a single hair to our heads,
even though it does not add a single inch to our heights,
I worry that silence itself is death
believing not that the lilies neither toil nor spin, at least a bit,

Christ
and him crucified
would the universe have been better for his timely silence
had that silence come before the silence that stilled Pilate,
had the bread not been broken, the cup not been drunk,
the choice that was no choice not been made,
the poetry that was no poetry not been written,
poetry that became words that became you and you again
you as you are, poetry altering the verb,
you as you might be because of this word:

Death In The Pot

"As they began to eat the stew, they cried out, "O man of God,
there is death in the pot!" And they could not eat it. Elisha said,
"Get some flour. "He put it into the pot and said, "Serve it to the
people to eat." And there was nothing harmful in the pot.":
        2 Kings 4 40:41

"That'll learn you"
was preaching in my heart
as I keeked out the December window
and thick flakes of snow falling softly, snow on snow,
and I could see the distant red glow of your cigarette burning
as you stood outside the church door, and you alone, cold, early,
waiting for the Christmas dance.

The Christmas dance:
what a beautiful tune it is in my head now,
remembering Easdale and the ringleted girls,
the whooping nights, the swans on the wide moonlit firth,
the Aurora Borealis, evening into night into day,
and in the distance day is dawning
I can see the early morning,
something tells me that I'm going home.

Going home:
what a wonderful chorus it is in my head now,
remembering Oban and the summer holidays,
the days in the long bracken, the fishing boats out of Cuan,
the footballing nights, summer into autumn into winter,
and in the distance now that night
and your cigarette and the red glow
and the hard poison of my heart.

My heart:
what a sweet aroma arises from it now,
herbs and spices, cinnamon and incense and myrrh,
memories of Mull, your brown legs crossed in the park,
passing you on the boat in Castlebay, kissing you in Tiree,
a night playing football in Luing, driving through Perthshire,
eating paella with you in Spain, sliding in the snow,
crying, gold, frankincense and myrrh: the perfect gifts.

The perfect gifts:
O God, how imperfect they really were, tarnished and hesitant,
selfish, confused, all guilty and all innocent
as if I can't remember whether my father was as kind as he was,
as loving as he was, as gentle as he was, and the summer sun
then
different, elongated and hopeful
even as this poem is despite itself
and the evening sun now precise and dated, aged exactly thirty-
seven.

What kept me looking at you
and you out there alone in the snow
was nothing else but fear:
when all else is taken away, it is sheer stark terror,
lack of love again and again and again,
though if you put a coat on it perhaps it was pride
that, whatever else I was suffering,
at least I was not out there alone,
a red glow waiting for a Christmas dance:
that really is fear.

I have been   all my life.
I have been so   in the middle of all the swaying corn,
in the land of the marram-grass in the land of the barley,
in the land of the ever-young
when old-fashioned haystacks were made I was
one day when I was about seven we sailed for Eriskay and I was
isolated in paradise, without love in rustic wonder,
                              when I married, when I scored those goals,
when I saw you walking by, when I wrote these poems,
I was there,   , with you and your cigarette glowing red.

It is no wonder
that I now believe
that there was a man of sorrows, acquainted with grief,
pierced for my transgressions, crushed for my iniquities,
suffering my suffering, sorrowing my sorrow,   my
and him a Gael, not opening his mouth
except to exclaim : "It is finished."

Out Of The Mine

Air   Light   Sky

Air bright air heady air clear

Light bright light shining light crystal

Sky bright sky blue sky clear

Air, light, sky:

Air   Light   Sky

"I see people; they look like trees walking around."

I see people; they look like trees walking around: miners with
satchels going home, brick houses on the horizons, the women at
the washing, boys playing football on the hillside.

Is this a 1950's film, or am I going home, out of the mine?
James Mason and Lawrence,
Lowry and the thin sketches,
Stan Barstow and the struggles, a very part of my corpuscles.

These men fly around me, running,
black dust in their hair, black boots pounding, running,
the distant smoke beckoning, the football pools,
each miner calling "See you Monday, Angus".

Already, looking down on my home and my unlatched gate, on my
wife behind the curtain and my daughter completing her jigsaw on
the kitchen table I have forgotten this:

Air   Light   Sky

Air light up there in the blue blue sky,
coal dust brushes off my chapped hands,
dropping on to the green grass:

Air   Light   Sky

I'll tell you something, lad: this town was built on pain - dank
houses without air, tiny bedrooms without light, basement
kitchens without sky, rich seams, rich rich seams of pain and
anguish and black Biblical truths.

As they jog home
the satchels clap their backs,
huppity, huppity, huppity, hup, hup, hup,
"See you Monday, Angus", "See you Monday, Angus", "See you
Monday, Angus".

Air, light, sky,
and because of it I know nothing anymore:
air, some say, was Saturday afternoon and the football,
light, some say, was Saturday evening and the pigeons,
sky, some say, was Saturday night and a bit of beer,

and I,
gold nuggets of Ophir at the rich, painful fronts,
the thrill of fresh coal, the immense jewels of darkness,
the excitement of coming out of the shaft, glimpses of air, light
and sky,
Saturday evenings with my family, trips by train to the city,
a picnic in the meadows when our daughter was born, willow
baskets and fruit,
then the black seams again, the richness, the darkness, the
fruitfulness,
penance for the light air in the sky,
a balance for my sins, a reason for my existence

until the seam was finished, the mine closed,
and there on the surface was air, light and sky
and everyone going home, satchels on their backs,
whistling, the wives at the washing, the boys playing football on
the hill,
the girls playing marbles on the pavement, the whistles blowing
and the smell of tea, pie and potatoes, in the Yorkshire air.

Interpreting The Dream

"This mystery has been revealed to me, not because I have greater
wisdom than other living men, but so that you, O king, may know
the interpretation and that you may understand what went through
your mind.":   The Book of Daniel (2:30)

The sixth funeral in a fortnight,
and all of them young men:
one drowned, one hanged, one at the foot of the stairs,
one in bed, one in a chair, and one that I have added,
a dream, perplexing the king:

in the dream were names, Alasdair Dhòmhnaill Chorodail,
Alasdair Aonghais 'Ac Dhomhnaill, Eoghainn Chailean,
Peigi Chailean, Domhnall Bhròdaidh, Domhnall Eachainn,
Domhnall 'Ic Neill, names that I heard in a hut
while the barley grew, the horses snorted, a flower
known as bròg-na-cuthaige grew blue in April,
plovers nests hidden in folds of grass and
lilies yellow, white, floated deep out of reach, and
on September mornings sometimes you would come home
smelling of wood-shavings and faraway villages,
Bornish, Milton, Iochdar, Howmore, Lochskipport,

then a boat sailed, Galilean Minch, Coll on the horizon,
Colonsay, Tiree, Mull and places etched in scripture:
the Isle of Seil, Crianlarich, Arthur's Seat, Jericho,
Mesopotomia, Mombasa, thin booklets telling of a career at sea
and how Table Mountain looked on a July morning,
Auckland in August, Cairo in January, cousins in Australia

then the kingdoms coming, clay, iron, bronze, silver, gold,
head, chest, arms, belly, thighs, legs, feet a statue

awesome, drug filled, powerful, majestic, remarkable,
reaching unto the very ends of the earth, then divided,
broken to pieces, swept away, chaff
on a threshing-floor in the summer sun

and the ancient memories still there:
how I never broke any of the fragile eggs,
how the dogs barked, how the cattle grazed,
how your unshaven cheek smelt oil and wood
creosote, paint, the dirt under your fingernails
a rock in the back of my mind, looped, caught,
anchored, your huge palms caressing my hair,
and my sister Mary standing in a purple frock
age four, or five, or six, or seven, my love
there is a sheep-worn path down to the river
where Palm Sundays walked, where stones rolled,
where boats sailed paper-grey and wood-white
rolling tumbling, avoiding, careering, over
the one-foot waterfall to the bay like
one of those extinguished stars that we still see
writing, in lucid finger, on the plaster of the sky:

Mene, Mene, Tekel, Parsin;
Mene, Mene, Tekel, Parsin;

Cuinnte, Cuinnte, Gann, Geairrte;
Cuinnte, Cuinnte, Gann, Geairrte;

Numbered, Weighed, Found Wanting, Divided;
Numbered, Weighed, Found Wanting, Divided;

the detached fingers of a human hand writing on the wall
and I, here called Belteshazzer,
called to interpret a Babylonian dream,

an imprisonment, a furnace, a lion's den,
an exile, a Scotland beyond repair,
an afterthought, death and yet more death,
one funeral after another, one drinking binge after another,
red cars, red tractors, red curtains,
the house of Dòmhnall Mairi Anndra,
the house of Dòmhnall Bàn Eachainn,
the house of Tàillear Illesbuig,
my own home at Foveran, the first time I saw you in the
playground,
the old pier at Achnacloich
the green jersey you wore in the rain,
the meal we had the day I graduated,
the night you died, that day we parted,
ships, boats, trains, buses, typewriters, pens, orders,
kisses, lust, blossom, numbered, weighed, found wanting, divided,
mene, mene, tekel, parsin, cuinnte, cuinnte, gann, geairrte,

and the days numbered, whether time or time and a half,
the dreams counted, interpreted,
that cottage and the many peat banks cut,
that cottage and the many cattle taken to market,
that cottage and the oldest son a doctor,
that cottage and that cottage and that cottage
until the vision is literal, until the fourth man is seen,
until humility is raised on high, until poetry itself dies.

Windows

Angus MacIsaac now lives in Southampton.
"He's married and has a good job", my mother said, after his
mother's funeral.
I wasn't there, when it mattered.

He sits beside me in the classroom,
a boy I loved for his abilities as an inside forward.
When play-time came and the teams were picked we were there,
side by side:
inside-forward, centre-forward, goal.

Southampton. South Hampton.

Their house stood high on a rocky hill above the Sound of Eriskay.
Rocks were there for slipping on,
for sliding on a fun-filled winter's day.
I can't remember, but there would have been toys:
bicycles, spinning tops, coloured crayons.

After me, he would have been the best football player in the
school.

I remember my father sitting in his mother's kitchen once
and they were laughing. Tea brewed.
We played.
My father had installed new windows for her and she was pleased.
The windows, I know now, would have measured two feet by two, a
holy universe.

Dear father, dead building the world, dear Mrs MacIsaac, dear
Angus, how I loved you.

Treasure Trove

"For where your treasure is, there your heart will be also." Jesus
Christ in The Sermon on the Mount (Matthew 6:21).

Home is the sailor, home from the sea,
with this inlaid grained chest from Macau,
this tinkling silver ballerina from Cairo,
this postcard from Rio, this stamp from the South Seas
this badge from the butterfly farm, this letter from Assam,
this kiss from Iceland, this memory from Kyle,
this dress from C&A's, this poem from Edinburgh:

> **Catriona**
>
> *I never knew you*
> *but I've seen those like you*
> *in spotted frocks and warm folds of flesh,*
> *always sweeping, and quietly making tea,*
> *always on hot hot summer evenings -*

a poem I wrote sixteen years ago,
and the rest of the lines either forgotten or unworthy:
what I remember now are old thatched houses and sand on the
floor,
cats in the tiny windows and flies and dogs sniffing at your heels,
and old clocks ticking away and the speckled dust
and the music of the kettle and the barley of the tea,
scones, jam, and each and everyone of these people now dead,
the patterned aprons finally laid down, the black boots curled in
dung-heaps,
the occasional face remembered, wrinkled, hands brushing flour
across blue,
food appeared, tea pouring, rocks glinting, laughs laughing,
iron stoves, fish smells, cream Rayburns, perhaps a sweetie:
Catriona by the stove

and the husbands, the men, at sea
swarthy, black, creosoted, pungent,
gathering the grained chests from Macau,
the silver ballerinas, the postcards, the stamps:
from the promontory at Glendale you could see Calvay
washed by high white waves
and the sudden sea-changes turning Eriskay into a mist,
Orosay invisible, Barra Head the wrath of the winter storm
and somehow, even then, knowing that men drowned,
whether at drunken pier-heads in Oban or lashed
by Arctic ices in places that my classroom head rang -
what remains are fragments that stunned:
my sister Mary gashing her head on a barbed-wire fence,
Alex the Insurance Man falling off his motorbicycle,
cries in the Uist silence and my parents
telling me how one night they heard a motorbicycle
revving, dying, the very moment my cousin Donald was killed
ashore on leave in Melbourne, merchant navy deaths
and most of the houses decorated by geography:
clocks from Singapore, calendars from Canada,
dolls from Port Said, perfume from Liverpool,
photographs of ships, sea-songs on cassettes
and those massive women, Anna, Catriona, Mairi, awash in flour
and the men now home and lying on the braes, in the sun,
wet clods cut thick, peat smack on dull wet grass, milk, tea, whisky,
sun glinting windows, dogs, ends of houses, sunlight on firth, lamps,
candles, comics gathered, Vespucci in the classroom,
Magellan, da Gama, the Bosphorus, the Niagara Falls

and how small were the gathered treasures, the sold lives,
the many poor Highlanders sacrificed as cannon-fodder by the
British Army,
dead in the Napoleonic Wars, dead in India, dead in Canada,

dead in America, dead in Europe, dead in Ireland
for the summer's evening reward of a treasured memory amidst the flour,
a commendation from Ypres, a note of sorrow from London,
a poem from me, perhaps a picture or a letter from a relative
making life a treasure trove tolerated
for where else could the heart be but wherèver the treasure was scattered,
fragments in Uist and fragments in Australia,
fragments in Inverness and fragments in Edinburgh

gathered for you, my treasure, from the world's end,
from every dusty port that a Uistman ever saw
simply for the memory of flour and Catriona
and you, my love, the very heart of all flour and coming memory.

Cover design, photography and drawing by Lyndsay M Howieson.